The
"Divine
Impatience"

The "Divine Impatience"

Speeches from
the First Fatima Peace Conference

Part I, II, III Copyright © 2000 *The Fatima Crusader*

Appendix I, II Copyright © 2000 *The Fatima Crusader*

Appendix III, Copyright © 2000, Christopher Ferrara, Esq.

Front Cover artwork: Joan Hoffsommer

ISBN 1-896384-04-8

Publisher:
Immaculate Heart Publications
U.S.A. - Box 1028, Buffalo, New York 14205
Canada - Box 602, Fort Erie, Ontario L2A 5X3
Printed in U.S.A.

THE "DIVINE IMPATIENCE"

Part I

THE URGENCY OF THE FATIMA MESSAGE

Part II

THE WINDOW OF OPPORTUNITY

Part III

THE "DIVINE IMPATIENCE"

Appendices

Contributors

Father Nicholas Gruner, *S.T.L., S.T.D., (Cand.),* heads one of the largest Fatima Apostolates in the world. He publishes *The Fatima Crusader,* and also produces the Television program "Fatima: 'the Moment has Come' " and the radio program, "Heaven's Peace Plan".

Father Marcel Nault (RIP) preacher, pastor and fervent apostle of Our Lady of Fatima and of the Holy Face of Jesus.

Father Paul Leonard Kramer, *B.Ph., S.T.B., M. Div., S.T.L.(Cand.),* author of numerous articles on the subject of Fatima, and of the book *A Theological Vindication of Roman Catholic Traditionalism.*

Father Paul Trinchard, holds a licentiate in Sacred Theology and Masters Degree in both Philosophy and Physics. He is author of numerous books including *The Awesome Fatima Consecration, God's Word,* and *The Abbot and Me on Liturgy.*

Coralie Graham is editor of *The Fatima Crusader.*

Deirdre Manifold, from Galway, Ireland, has authored numerous books including *Fatima and the Great Conspiracy, Karl Marx: True or False Prophet,* and *Towards World Government.*

Josyp Terelya from Ukraine has fought the cause of Catholicism all his life. He spent 20 years in prisons and detention camps in Communist Russia, which is detailed in his autobiography, *Witness to Apparitions and Persecution in the USSR.*

Introduction

In October of 1992, an historic event took place at Fatima, Portugal. It was here that *The Fatima Crusader* hosted its first International Bishops Conference, which represented one of the largest private gatherings of Catholic bishops in history and the first ever convened for the express purpose of discussing details of the famous Fatima apparitions. This book contains the speeches presented at this Conference. These speeches were all recorded electronically and later transcribed. They have been edited slightly for readability while remaining faithful to the thought of the speakers.

The Fatima Crusader is the journal of the International Fatima Rosary Crusade, and is wholly dedicated to promoting devotion to and interest in the full Message of Our Lady of Fatima. The magazine's founder, Father Nicholas Gruner, is known to millions through this publication, as well as through his daily television and radio programs.

When asked why *The Fatima Crusader* sponsors these Peace Conferences, Father Gruner gives three reasons:

1) In 1931, Our Lord told Sister Lucy, the lone surviving seer of Fatima, "Make it known to My ministers given that they follow the example of the king of France in delaying the execution of My command, like him they will follow him into misfortune." Our Lord wants this Fatima Message to be known by His ministers, that is, by His bishops. As Our Lord's words indicate, there are dire consequences for not heeding Heaven's request.

2) The late Hamish Fraser of Scotland, editor of *Approaches* magazine, was a zealous apostle of Fatima. He related that Sister Lucy remarked

that many bishops need to be *catechized* regarding the Fatima Message.

3) In 1980, in the presence of Cardinal Wyszinski of Poland, Pope John Paul II said that those who are seeking the fulfillment of Our Lady's requests—especially the Consecration of Russia for world peace—should first go to the bishops to seek their support and assistance.

Hence, in bringing the Fatima Message directly to the bishops, *The Fatima Crusader* is merely following the directives of Our Lord, Sister Lucy and Pope John Paul II.

Father Gruner's apostolate is one that has sparked controversy, primarily because of its steadfast promotion of the *full* Message of Fatima, which insists on two aspects of the Fatima Message that many have deemed bothersome:

1) That the Third Secret, which was supposed to have been released in 1960, be revealed in its entirety.

2) The urgent necessity for the Collegial Consecration of Russia to the Immaculate Heart of Mary by the Pope in union with all the bishops throughout the world.

The violence that controversy is capable of fomenting was visited upon this 1992 Conference. The local bishop, who was holding his own conference at the time, denounced *The Fatima Crusader's* Conference as operating "without ecclesiastical permission," even though no such permission is required.

Because of the subsequent confusion generated in the Press by officials of the Fatima Shrine, about 25 bishops and Archbishops met in the afternoon on October 7, 1992, with Father Gruner to have their questions answered regarding the Bishops Peace Conference scheduled to start the following morning.

Having been satisfied, they decided to seek an audience with the then local bishop, His Excellency Bishop Alberto Cosme do Amaral of Fatima. Three Archbishops, one from India, one from the Philippines and one from Brazil, went as representing the other bishops. At 9 p.m. they met the local bishop who lived in Leiria, 18 kilometers away. This meeting lasted several hours.

Despite the fact that the former Bishop of Fatima, Bishop Alberto, had been the source of grossly misleading statements about Father Gruner and the Bishops Peace Conference, he nonetheless agreed to make the Peace Conference an official part of the Fatima Shrine's Conference which Bishop Alberto himself was hosting.

Even though, as Canon Law experts among participants at the Bishops Peace Conference stated, there was no need to have the official invitation and official status granted by the local bishop, this unexpected turn of events was indeed welcomed by all. Especially as it provided a particularly strong response to the misrepresentations published about the international Conference in the daily and international press.

This accord was announced by the Archbishops returning from Leiria at about midnight to the organizers of the Peace Conference and was then publicly announced from the podium the next day at the opening session by His Grace Archbishop José Cardoso Sobrinho, Archbishop of Recife, Brazil.

Yet despite this apparent truce, Father Gruner, while in the sacristy of the Capelinha, was the victim of a sudden, unprovoked physical attack by Shrine workers on October 10. The details of this attack at the 1992 Conference are outlined in *Fatima Priest,* the story of Father Gruner and his Fatima apostolate.

The following pages contain superb presentations by respected Catholic scholars, writers and pastors who support the truth that the *full* Fatima Message must be known and promptly obeyed. The reader will note that many of the speeches contain a note of urgency, as speakers of various expertise explain the full gravity of the Fatima Message, without ambiguity and without apology. The hour is late and the consequences momentous. Nonetheless, this book is also one of hope. The solution to world disorder caused by sin is easily within reach. It is only for us to submit ourselves to Our Lady's simple, loving directives.

The speeches are divided into three sections according to their respective themes. The book closes with five appendices that include a letter from Bishop Arulappa on the need for the Collegial Consecration, encouragement from various bishops, and also a commentary on one of the most bizarre episodes ever to occur in the ongoing Fatima drama.

At the time of this 1992 Peace Conference, two prelates and a Portuguese-speaking priest from the Conference were present at an interview with Sister Lucy conducted by Mr. Carlos Evaristo, in which "Sister Lucy" apparently denied a substantial portion of what she has been saying for the past 70 years. This interview, subsequently published under the name of "Two Hours with Sister Lucy", has been the source of immeasurable confusion.

Since this encounter was indirectly related to the 1992 Fatima Conference, the publishers have included a brilliant rebuttal of the interview by attorney Christopher Ferrara, which exposes the interview as fraudulent and deliberately misleading.

The publication of this book is of great importance. Through its pages, the work of this historic Conference lives on. By it, the vast number of concerned Faithful who could not attend these seminars may nevertheless benefit from the superb lectures presented. It is hoped that this work will enkindle in many souls a renewed commitment to the *full* Message of Fatima.

Part I
The
Urgency
of the
Fatima Message

Chapter 1

The Profound Simplicity and Urgent Worldwide Importance of the Real Fatima Message

by Father Nicholas Gruner

A Profound Message

"If mankind does not amend then God will punish the world by four punishments: war, hunger, persecution of the Church and persecution of the Holy Father."

All of us can understand war and famine as a punishment for the sins of the world, but very few of us can understand persecution of the Church as a punishment for the sins of the world. The Blessed Virgin did not say that as punishment for the sins of the Church, God would allow the persecution of the Church. Rather, She said that for the punishment of the sins of mankind, the Church would be persecuted. The Church today suffers persecution as one of the four chastisements of the world. It is this very persecution of the Church that impedes the fulfillment of Our Lady's request.

It is precisely because sin is so great, as Pope John Paul II pointed out at Fatima, that the world has gone in the opposite direction from Our Lady's Message of 1917. Sin has been enthroned. Sin has been institutionalized in the world. As a result, the Church herself is persecuted. The net effect has been that within the Church Our Lady's requests have not been understood, have not been heard, have not been obeyed and have not been loved as Our Lady expected them to be.

3

The Profound Simplicity of Her Message

The things Our Lady said are so simple they tend to pass us by. We think we understand what She is saying when we really do not. That is not only due to our slowness of wit, our slowness of understanding, but it is also due to the fact that the Message of Fatima has been partly hidden.

It has been hidden as a result, first of all, of the devil's attack and, secondly, as a result of human "diplomacy". For example, when, in 1942, the second part of the Secret was published, so as not to offend the Allies during the War, the word "Russia" was taken out of the secret and replaced by terms like "evil forces".

The Message of Fatima is very difficult to, as the Italians say, *Inquadrare,* put a framework around because, in part, we are standing in the middle of the picture. We are not far enough away to recognize it. Yet the Message of Our Lady of Fatima is more important than anything in the last one thousand years of the Church's history, including all the councils, all the other apparitions of Our Lady, any world event, any war.

The Message of Our Lady of Fatima may, in fact, be contained in Sacred Scripture. Her appearance at Fatima may well be predicted in the Bible. Pope Paul VI suggested this in his encyclical *Signum Magnum* of May 13, 1967. The Apocalypse (12:1) reads, "I saw the Woman clothed with the sun, with the moon under Her feet, and the crown of twelve stars on Her head." In this encyclical, the Pope clearly, deliberately and very strongly suggests that the Woman of the Apocalypse is none other than Our Lady of Fatima.

Sister Lucy tells us Our Lady is sad because no one pays attention to Her Message, neither the good nor the bad. The bad go their way not seeing their chastisement falling on them. The good, also, pay no attention to the

Message. Unfortunately, it is still true that even today the good still do not give much attention nor importance to Her Message.

To put the full Fatima Message in context it is important to remember Our Lady promised that, "In the end, My Immaculate Heart will triumph." This triumph will be much greater than any of us can fully understand. But the triumph will come in three parts. The first part is, "In the end, My Immaculate Heart will triumph. The Holy Father will consecrate Russia to Me." The second part is, "Russia will be converted." The third part is, "A period of peace will be given to mankind."

Conversion and Peace

In using these words, the Blessed Virgin is using them in the Catholic sense, of conversion. She speaks of the conversion of Russia to the Catholic Faith. When She speaks about peace being given to the world She is speaking in the terms that Christ tells us, "I give you peace but not as the world gives it." This peace She is talking about is not just the absence of war so we can spread more of Western consumerism. It is a period of Christian peace. First of all, a peace of the heart and soul, for this peace will extend to society, in all aspects of it. This peace can only come about through the reign of Christ the King. As Pope Pius XI explained in his encyclical *Quas Primas* on Christ the King, He is the King of rulers, as Scripture tells us, He is King of Kings and Lord of Lords. This kingship that we pray for when we say "Thy Kingdom Come" in the Our Father will be recognized and realized in this reign of peace. The Catholic Church will be recognized as the One, True Church founded by Jesus Christ. The role of the bishops and the role of the Holy Father will be enhanced, will be recognized, will be supported. We will see the realization of the prophecies of glory. As it says in Isaiah, "Let us go on to the mountain of God to see what the Lord has done." But in order for this to happen there must first occur a dramatic event. That "something dramatic" will be the consecration of Russia as Our Lady requested it.

This consecration has to be something very public, otherwise the faithful and the non-believers will not recognize it. It cannot be merely something done in a chapel privately, all by yourself. That would, of course, be a holy act of prayer pleasing to God. But for the fulfillment of this request to be dramatic and effective it has to be public and solemn. This is clear from the very nature of the promise given and the very nature of the way the request was given. Let us take an exact look at how the request was given.

It occurred in the most solemn of all Our Lady of Fatima's visions and took place at Tuy which is on the border of Spain and Portugal. Lucy had permission to pray before the Blessed Sacrament in the evening on her own, in the manner of Saint Margaret Mary Alacoque. It was midnight. The chapel was entirely in darkness except for the vigil light. All of a sudden, the whole chapel was illuminated with a supernatural light. She looked up and saw Our Lady standing on the altar on a little cloud. She saw the Son of God on the Cross. Over the head of God the Son was God the Holy Spirit in the form of a dove and above that, God the Father in the form of an older man. Under the right arm of Christ, the Eucharist came from the wound in His side. Blood dripped from the Eucharist into the chalice which was suspended in the air just below the Eucharist. The Immaculate Heart of the Blessed Virgin was shown surrounded by thorns. In Her hand She held the Rosary. Underneath the left arm of Our Lord were written three words in water-like form. They said, "Grace and Mercy".

At this point Our Lady spoke. She said, "The moment has come in which God asks the Holy Father to make and to command all the Catholic Bishops of the world to make the consecration of Russia."

God Wants to Exalt the Pope and Bishops

The reason the request for the consecration of Russia must be done in the manner that God has specified is because God wants to exalt not only the Blessed Virgin but He also wants to exalt, in the eyes of the whole world, the Holy Father. When the world realizes that peace has come through the obedience of the Holy Father and the bishops, the world will be grateful not only to the Blessed Virgin and Her Immaculate Heart but also to the Pope and the bishops.

All of us have been secularized in our thinking about how society should function. We might expect peace to be maintained or upheld by the great armies of the United States or the United Nations' Peacekeeping Forces. Others might look to Moscow.

There is a dogmatic truth which was solemnly defined by Pope Boniface VIII, around the year 1300 A.D. that there are two authorities, the temporal and the spiritual, and these two authorities come from God.

In addition there is a relationship between these two authorities and that is, the spiritual is superior to the temporal and the temporal must be subject to it. He defined it in the terms of the two swords that Peter held. The temporal sword and the spiritual sword.

Today some of us might translate "temporal authority" into "secular authority", but very clearly, we cannot use the language of the secularists which defines secularism as "of this world and this world alone."

"Secular authority" by its very definition denies the rights of God over temporal affairs. It shows how far we have gotten away from this truth of the Catholic Faith. And this truth that Boniface VIII proclaimed will be re-affirmed when temporal peace is given through the spiritual authority being exercised by the Holy Father and by the bishops under the direction of the Queen of Heaven and the Queen of Peace.

Yes to God, Christ and Church

This peace that She refers to will reverse the great wounds that the Church has endured from 1054, 1517, 1717 and 1917. It was Pius XII who pointed out that in 1517 Luther said, "Yes" to God, "Yes" to Christ and "No" to the Church. In 1717 the Freemasons surfaced in London and said "Yes" to God, "No" to Christ and "No" to the Church. In 1917 the Communists said "No" to God, "No" to Christ and "No" to the Church. It is to reverse these three "No's"; the "No" to the Church, the "No" to Christ and the "No" to God that Our Lady came in 1917.

Through the conversion of Russia to the Catholic Faith and the subsequent missionary activity of a converted Catholic Russia, the rest of the world will be converted. We cannot have the peace of Christ in the whole world without the conversion of the world to the Catholic Faith.

And so the "No" of Marx will be, in fact, converted to "Yes." "Yes" to God, "Yes" to Christ and "Yes" to the Church. And the "No" of the Masons who say "No" to the Church and "No" to Christ will be turned into "Yes." And the "No" of the Protestants who have said "No" to the Church will be turned to "Yes." And the "No" of the Orthodox who in 1054 said "No" to the Pope will also be turned to "Yes" to the Pope. The results of saying "Yes" to Our Lady will be the world saying "Yes" to God, "Yes" to Christ, "Yes" to the Church and "Yes" to the Pope.

It is a total conversion Our Lady speaks about. It is not an ecumenical conversion as was conceived of by some after 1965. Such an idea is actually contrary to what the Second Vatican Council says. "The Decree on Ecumenism" says that the greatest work of ecumenism is to convert people to the Catholic Faith. The Council, in paragraphs fourteen to eighteen of *Lumen Gentium* (the Constitution in the Church) still affirms the doctrine that outside the Church there is no salvation, contrary to what many of the popularizers of the Council say.

God Wants to Establish in the World Devotion to the Immaculate Heart of Mary

These truths which have been largely forgotten will be understood through grace and through the action of the Blessed Virgin. The role of the Blessed Virgin Herself will be better understood. After studying the Message of Fatima for many years, it is clear that in the mind of God, true devotion to the Blessed Virgin has never been fully established in the Church from the beginning until the present.

That conclusion is based on the phrase Our Lady said on July 13, 1917. "You have seen hell, where the souls of poor sinners go. In order to save them, God wishes to establish in the world devotion to My Immaculate Heart." "God wishes to establish" means that, up until now, He has not established in the world devotion to the Immaculate Heart.

That is not to say that there have not been great Saints and great devotion to Our Lady in the past or even in the present. However, in the world, this devotion has not been sufficiently established. And God wants to establish this devotion. The reason for establishing this devotion is explained. God wants to save sinners. That is His primary purpose and to accomplish this purpose God will establish devotion to Our Lady.

Saint Alphonsus Liguori tells us it has never been known that anyone who persisted in his devotion to the Blessed Virgin has ever been lost and he confirms this same teaching of Saint Bernard in his book, *The Glories of Mary*. God wants to establish in the world devotion to the Immaculate Heart of Mary in our time.

The Blessed Virgin said at Fatima, "Only I can help you." Some Protestants have raised the objection, "Is the Blessed Virgin more important than God?" Of course, the answer is No. Nevertheless, through the plan of God Himself, God has entrusted the peace of the world to Her Immaculate Heart.

God Himself will not give us this peace except through the merits and intercession of the Blessed Virgin and that is why the Blessed Virgin can say, "Only I can help you." Saint Augustine tells us that God, in His great love and His great Mercy towards mankind, wants to give certain favors and certain graces to us even though He knows we do not deserve them.

Nevertheless, God wants to give them to us despite our unworthiness but He also knows how weak we are and how prone we are to pride. He wants us also to understand that it is not through our own merits. That is why God will grant certain favors and graces only through the merits and intercession of the Saints. That is also why, at Fatima, we are told that the peace of the world has been entrusted exclusively to the Immaculate Heart of Mary.

Further, when Sister Lucy asked Our Lord why He would not bring peace to the world and convert Russia without the Holy Father and the bishops making the act of consecration, Our Lord did not say, "You misunderstand, My daughter, I do not mean that literally." On the contrary, He confirmed Sister Lucy's understanding and gave the reason. He said it is because, "I want My whole Church to recognize that consecration as a triumph of the Immaculate Heart of Mary, thereby later on, placing devotion to My Mother's Immaculate Heart beside devotion to My Own Sacred Heart.

WORLDWIDE IMPORTANCE

Russia Will Spread Her Errors

Most of you are aware that the Russian Revolution was inspired by Marx but many of you perhaps do not know that Marx was a satanist. He wrote poetry in which he expressed that he had sold his soul to the devil and that from Hell he would hurl curses upon mankind. Father Paul Leonard explains Marx's poetry in great length in the introduction to my book, *World Enslavement or Peace ... It's Up To The Pope.*

Every one of the Ten Commandments of God are opposed by the "ten commandments" of Marxism. For example, in opposition to the Eighth Commandment, "Thou Shalt Not Bear False Witness Against Thy Neighbor", Lenin said, "The lie is sacred." Our Lord speaks of the devil as a murderer and a liar from the beginning and Lenin/Marxism tells us that "the lie is sacred."

In opposition to God's Seventh Commandment, "Thou Shalt Not Steal", Marx tells us no one has a right to private property and commands his followers, "Steal anything you can."

In the Fifth Commandment we are told, "Thou Shalt Not Kill." Many people do not realize the institutionalizing of abortion came from Russia. It was not legal in any

11

country until the early 1920's. Today legalized abortion kills fifty million babies each year, and that is a conservative estimate. Scripture tells us this is one of the four crimes that cry to Heaven for vengeance and chastisement. When Our Lady spoke about the errors of Russia She did not speak about the errors of Marx and Lenin but about Russia. She said they would be spread throughout the world. Abortion is the clearest example of what She meant.

20th Century Apostasy Predicted

Cardinal Ratzinger tells us that the Third Secret of Fatima, which he assures us he has read, refers to the last times and is contained in Sacred Scripture. He also tells us that the Third Secret refers to the dangers to the Faith and therefore to the life of the Christian and therefore to the life of the world. When we remember that Sister Lucy tells us the Third Secret is in Apocalypse, Chapters 8 to 13, we realize it is difficult to exaggerate the terrible dangers of the times in which we are living.

We must recognize how close we are to the edge of the precipice. During Our Lady's appearance at Quito, Ecuador, in 1634, She predicted our times. She said the Church would cede, give way to persecution, to heresy for the latter part of the 19th Century and most of the 20th. There are only eight years left in the 20th Century.

From the prophecy of Our Lady at Quito, Our Lady of Good Fortune, a prophecy approved by the Church, we are given to understand that the heresy that is spreading through the Church will be overcome by the year 2000. Cardinal Ratzinger tells us that the Faith is in danger around the world.

Jesus' Frightful Prophetic Warning to Bishops

The big question before us today is, will this triumph of Our Lady over heresy be through a bloodbath or will it be totally peaceful, brought about by listening to Our Lady of Fatima in time? Our Lord, speaking to Sister Lucy in August of 1931, gave her a message, and messages like this are very painful for her to deliver.

It was just two years and two months after the Blessed Virgin came in 1929 to fulfill Her promise to ask for the consecration of Russia. At that time, June 13, 1929, She said, "The moment has come in which God asks the Holy Father to make and to command all the bishops of the world to make the consecration of Russia to My Immaculate Heart. God promises to save Russia by this means. So numerous are the souls which justice condemns for sins committed against Me that I come to ask for Reparation."

In 1931, just two years and two months later, Our Lord came back to say, "Make it known to My ministers, given that they follow the example of the King of France in delaying the execution of My command, like him they will follow him into misfortune." The King of France referred to is actually Louis XIV, Louis XV and Louis XVI. On June 17, 1689, the Sacred Heart gave a command to the King of France for him to consecrate his country, the Kingdom of France, in a solemn and public way to the Sacred Heart of Jesus.

The command was given through Saint Margaret Mary Alacoque. For one hundred years the Kings of France — that is Louis XIV, Louis XV and Louis XVI — did not obey. So on June 17, 1789, the King of France was stripped of his power by the Third Estate and four years later he was executed by the guillotine. Our Lord makes reference to this command to the King of France. It is a terrifying prophecy but it is a command that Our Lord Himself tells us we must make known.

Pope John Paul II
Knows He Has Not Yet Obeyed

The Holy Father, Pope John Paul II has, on various occasions, expressed his own thoughts on the consecration. Even before he was made Pope he and all the Polish bishops, on two different occasions, petitioned Pope Paul VI for the consecration. After he was elected Pope, the Bishops of Poland again made the same petition.

On May 13, 1982, John Paul II consecrated the world, then on May 19, he said in public in Saint Peter's Square that he did all he could under the current circumstances, acknowledging implicitly that he had not done everything.

He made his thoughts clear on March 25, 1984. Before making the consecration of the world on March 25, 1984, the Pope sent a letter to the bishops of the world. It was dated December 8, 1983. He published it in *L'Osservatore Romano* around February 17, 1984.

He also published the text of the consecration and he explained that, except for a few minor modifications, it was the same text as the one he used in 1982. What is most striking is that, on March 25, 1984, during the actual ceremony, he did follow the text but he made one significant variation. He acknowledged to Our Lady of Fatima before a quarter of a million people in Saint Peter's Square that what he was doing that day was not what Our Lady of Fatima had requested. After the act of consecration he said, "Enlighten especially the peoples of which You, Yourself, are awaiting our consecration and our entrusting." This was published the next day on the front page and page 6 in *L'Osservatore Romano*.

The verb in Italian is in the present tense. He thereby acknowledged that Our Lady was still waiting for the consecration of Russia, after he has consecrated the world.

In the afternoon, four hours later, he said it again inside Saint Peter's that Our Lady was still awaiting the consecration of a certain people. He said this to Our Lady of Fatima as he knelt before Her Fatima Statue.

He acknowledged that Our Lady of Fatima has asked for one thing: for the consecration of Russia. The Holy Father, subsequent to that, has said privately that he wants to do it but he is waiting for one thing ... the bishops.

This second comment was published in the Italian Bishops' newspaper, *Avvenire*, on page eleven, the next day.

Sister Lucy's Consistent Testimony for Over Fifty Years

Sister Lucy has spoken about this act of consecration for more than fifty years. One of the foremost writers on Fatima through whom we get access to the apostolate of Sister Lucy was William Thomas Walsh, a professor of History at Manhattanville College in New York. He wrote a number of books on history including *Isabella of Spain, The Last Crusader*. One of the last books he wrote before he died was *Our Lady of Fatima*. On page 221 of this book he reports his interview with Sister Lucy conducted on July 15, 1946.

He asked the question of Lucy, "At what stage of the prophecies are we in today?" And she said, "We are in the stage of Russia spreading her errors throughout the world."

He said, "Does that mean that Russia will enslave the whole world?" And she said, "Yes." Walsh was speaking to Lucy through the translator, Father Manuel Rocha. This translator has himself been published regarding the same interview in *The Wonders She Performs* (See *The Fatima Crusader* Issue 22, page 6).

Professor Walsh asked the question again to Father Rocha and the translator again asked Sister Lucy the question, "Does this mean Russia will overcome the whole world?" And Walsh added, "Does that include the United States of America?" And Sister Lucy said again, "Yes."

She explained on that same occasion that, "What God wants is the consecration of Russia." Remember the year in which she is speaking is 1946. It is four years after Pope Pius XII consecrated the world on October 31, by a radio message here in Fatima and again on December 8 in Rome. Twice in 1942, he consecrated the world to the Immaculate Heart of Mary and yet, in 1946, four years later, Sister Lucy tells us it is not what Our Lady of Fatima asked for.

Pope Pius XII consecrated Russia on July 7, 1952. You can read much of the text of that consecration in Frère Michels' book, *The Whole Truth About Fatima*, Volume III, *The Third Secret.* Yet, Sister Lucy tells us it still did not fulfill the request of Our Lady of Fatima, because in this case, the bishops did not join in. The bishops, however, at that point had not been asked.

Pope Paul VI, at the end of the third session of the Council, in front of all the bishops on November 21, 1964, consecrated the world. At the end of each of these consecrations there have been those people who would tell us that we have peace in the world, that the conversion of Russia has now begun. We have published against these errors, not to embarrass them, but to show that these errors happen time and again, and to defend the true Fatima Message, and the promise. After 1942, after 1952, after 1964, after each consecration, Sister Lucy very clearly said, "No", it has not fulfilled Our Lady's request.

Last year, when I was in India, I had to go through the military checkpoint in Tamil Nadu because many of the Tamil Tigers from Ceylon were using it for a base of operations for revolution. If we had stepped out of the van we could have been shot, as anyone else would have been for breaking through a military checkpoint.

So, you don't have to be told there is no peace in the world. Look at Yugoslavia, Croatia, Lebanon. The peace that Our Lady promises will at least be an absence of war. That has not been achieved yet.

In an interview given to the Apostolic Nuncio, Archbishop Sante Portalupi, on March 21, 1982, before the Holy Father came to Fatima, Sister Lucy again explained what is needed for the consecration. It must be a solemn act, a public act. It must be to the Immaculate Heart of Mary. It must be the consecration of Russia, specifically.

She explained that Russia is a well-defined territory and when the world sees the people in that territory converting to Christ, they will recognize this as the sign that has been predicted. The consecration of the world does not specify and distinguish one part of the world from the other, and the sign would not be seen through consecrating the world to the Immaculate Heart.

Again, after the consecration of May 13, 1982, she gave an official interview on March 19, 1983, again to Archbishop Sante Portalupi, and to other witnesses, that the consecration of the year before did not fulfill Our Lady's request. Again, after 1984, she said a number of times, privately, that it did not fulfill Our Lady's request. This was published in a number of publications including our own.

Our Lady's Simple and Easy Request

Relatively speaking, the request is very simple and easy. But it is perceived as being of great difficulty because of two factors. One is diplomacy, the other is perceived opposition on the part of the bishops. Contrary to what some Vatican officials think, 95% of the bishops would be happy to do the consecration if the Holy Father asked them to.

As you know, I have written to the bishops of the world about eight times now. Few bishops have expressed dissatisfaction or opposition to this idea. We have received signed declarations from over 400 bishops saying that they are willing to do the Act of Consecration when the Holy Father asks for it, and that does not include the others who have indicated their support in letters. But there are some in the Vatican who feel that maybe 20% or 30%, at the maximum, would oppose the Act of Consecration. I do not think anywhere near that many bishops would disobey.

The Consecration of Russia — Truly Historic

The Consecration of Russia is as dramatic as, or even more dramatic than, the action of Moses on the banks of the Red Sea. What would have happened to the people of God at that time if Moses chose not to obey God's command to extend his staff over the Red Sea when the army of their enemy was bearing down on them with swords drawn and chariots racing?

What would have happened had Moses not believed, not obeyed? I believe, certainly, that event took place. But I also believe it to be a symbol and a lesson meant to be followed by the people of God today.

Whether or not one believes that analysis, the fact is that God chose to give a simple command to one man to save the rest of the people, and God thereby demonstrated the authority of Moses and His own authority. Likewise, God wants to demonstrate the authority of the Pope and the bishops in a dramatic fashion through this act of consecration.

Some people have simplified the Message of Fatima to the point of saying that we are spreading superstition. One bishop in the United States, when he was asked to demonstrate it or withdraw his remark, he withdrew his remark. As the Bishop of Mysore said, "If you want peace, prepare for war." In this work of making the Fatima Peace Message known, we may need to prepare for more than one war.

The Message of Fatima is not "magic," as some have suggested. Neither is it superstition. We believe Our Lady of Fatima. Every word that She uses She means, and She means it very literally. When Sister Lucy tells us that, "Many times the Blessed Virgin told me and my cousins Jacinta and Francisco that God has chosen Russia as an instrument of chastisement to punish the whole world, if we do not beforehand obtain the conversion of that poor nation", it is very scriptural.

When the Babylonians conquered the Jews, and before they took them off into captivity, it was Jeremiah who told the people of that time, who believed the promises of God, that Jerusalem was the holy city. Many Catholics believe that since God promised to be with His Church for all times, that therefore this cannot happen.

Jesus' Promise to the Church

God promised to be with His Church, it is true, but He never promised that *we* would be with the Church. The Catholic Church in North Africa, at the time of Saint Augustine, was flourishing. One hundred years later it was wiped out and it has not recovered fifteen hundred years later. So, although Our Lord promised to be with His Church, He has not promised all of us, or our countries, that we will be with the Church.

The prophecy of the Third Secret of Fatima predicts the present apostasy, the falling away from the Faith of entire nations. Therefore, those nations and people that fall away from the Catholic Faith will no longer be with the Church. Bishop Cosme do Amaral himself, on September 10, 1984, in a public talk given at the Vienna Technical University said, "The Third Secret does not refer to SS missiles; it refers to dangers to the Faith", and he said, "It is true that the apostasy of a nation is much worse than the annihilation of a nation."

Obviously to annihilate a nation is only a temporal disaster, but the apostasy of a nation is a spiritual, eternal disaster for that nation. Bishop do Amaral also said, "It is true that the Faith is becoming weaker and weaker in Europe every day."

Our Response

Since the Fatima Message has been covered with many years of disinformation and has been misunderstood for so long and been ignored by so many, Our Lady is very sad. There are still many powerful people inside the Church and in the world who, knowingly or unknowingly, are obstructing Our Lady's plan for peace by their ignorance and by their spreading falsehoods against Her full Fatima Message. Jesus tells us in the Gospel to be careful not to be taken in by these snares of the devil. "Do not judge by appearances," He solemnly cautions.

Before the bishops can carry out the command of the Queen of Heaven they must first come to know it. They must study and meditate on Her words so they can do their part to fulfill Her solemn command. They must not be tricked into not doing their part. They have, after all, heard the terrible warning of Jesus, that they may be executed publicly by the enemies of the Church if the consecration is not done in time.

The bishops can consecrate their dioceses and countries to the Immaculate Heart of Mary. There have been marvels of grace wrought through these acts of consecration to the Immaculate Heart, especially when done in a solemn and public way by the bishops.

Such acts of consecration are no substitute for the great request for the consecration of Russia by all the bishops of the Catholic world on the same day, at the same time, together with the Pope. But they, nevertheless, are a very powerful means of promoting devotion to the Immaculate Heart and are, indeed, richly blessed by God.

We are grateful to His Holiness Pope John Paul II for his Act of Consecrating the world in 1984. As he himself has said publicly, it is not what Our Lady of Fatima requested, and She is still awaiting this act of consecration. In 1984, we pointed out how good this was for the Church while still awaiting the compliance with Our Lady's request for the solemn, public, fully collegial Act of Consecration of Russia. As a result of that Act of 1984, God has granted to the Church a window of opportunity wherein the Holy Father and all the bishops would find it quite easy to do the proper consecration of Russia.

But this grace, once won, will not last long. The door of this opportunity will soon close if not acted upon in the near future and then I very much fear the "annihilation of nations" and the "enslavement of the whole world" that Our Lady predicted will take place in our century if we do not obey.

Spread the Fatima Message in your diocese wherever you can. Start Rosary Crusades everywhere for the Church and for the Holy Father, have the Brown Scapular distributed by the hundreds and thousands and make Our Lady's words and request be heard and obeyed everywhere.

Chapter 2

The Hope of the World

by Father Paul Trinchard

T.S. Eliot said, "our thanks to the invisible college of the humble who through the ages have accomplished everything essential." It is thanks to the little dollars of the people in the United States that all of us are here, and we thank Father Gruner for giving them the opportunity to help us become more acquainted with the Fatima Message. It is only known in its fullness, or its authenticity by about 5% of the population. So we have a huge task in front of us.

Christ's Order

As you get older you see the Grace of God in your life. If God graces you to see it, be very thankful for it. By the Grace of the Holy Spirit, I spent a couple of months in Fort Erie, and that was enough for me to figure out what the message of Fatima was. The basis of this message, which we haven't explored enough, is that there is only one true Church — "Outside the Church there is no salvation." This is not a post-Vatican II heresy. It is a perennial dogma of the Roman Catholic Church. This is one of the key foundations of Fatima.

The Pope and you bishops are the hope of the world. It is an awful responsibility you have, but you are the hope of the world. As the Church goes, so is the world blessed, and that is the Message of Fatima. It's such a powerful thing, so very powerful. If the Pope obeys God's Fatima Message, the whole world will be blessed.

Do you know how many bishops we have here from North America? Zero. That's to be expected. The existential Church in the United States of America is totally

23

corrupt by the fault of the bishops, sometimes by their active participation in fostering heresy. Christ established such a strong Church that even in the Church's corruption, you still have Christ's order. It's amazing how even in its corruption, it is a tightly knit organization, and as the top goes, so goes the bottom. People who see their Church leaders are wrong and don't know what to do, end up going into different groups or following different priests that are mainly centered around the Tridentine Mass, because its theology is correct. They split into splinter groups. Now God gave the Catholic Church this organization, this unity. So even in its corruption, it still maintains this unity, and bishops will hesitate to be against bishops. But, as Anne Catherine Emmerich predicts, in the end times, bishops will be against bishops. That is what we should be preparing for.

We have a message of hope. In the end the Pope will obey the Blessed Virgin Mary, Russia will be consecrated, peace will be obtained through the Roman Catholic Church, the only one true Church. The revealed truth that "outside the Church there is no salvation" holds for society as well as individuals. This is the Message of Fatima.

Russia's Errors

The Message of Fatima has three parts. The first part concerns individuals, mostly to bring them back to sanity. There is also the dramatic reminder that there is a Hell and Hell is the only eternal evil. Don't be afraid to preach about Hell. Don't be ashamed of that. That is what Our Lady says in the first message, Hell is the only eternal evil, and sin is the only material present evil. It is sin that causes a soul to go to Hell.

The United States is already embracing Russia's errors. We have more of Russia's errors in the United States than Russia has. You can't mention Jesus Christ in our government schools in the United States. You can't put the Ten Commandments on the wall in our government schools. Yet in Russia you can mention Jesus now.

The United States has degenerated quite a lot. Now we've got hate laws. We've got things like the rights of children. "The rights of the child to play" may sound nice at first. "The right of the child for religion" may also sound nice at first. What it means in practice is that if the State decides that you are making your child take responsibilities, then the child will be taken away from you, because you violated his "right to play". If the State learns that your little ten-year-old doesn't want to go to Church anymore, but you are making her go anyway, then your child will be taken away from you, because you violated her "freedom of religion".

What are Russia's errors in general? Worshipping man in place of God. That is also the foundation of the United States government today. Worship of man in place of God. How that must certainly grieve the Sacred Heart of Jesus and the Immaculate Heart of Mary.

As the Pope goes, so goes the whole world. We have the promise that in the end the Immaculate Heart of Mary will conquer, Russia will be consecrated and a period of peace will be given to the world. Would to God that you and I will be part of getting that message out. Everybody will rejoice when the Church is as it should be, and the whole world will be blessed when the Pope does as he should do. There will be a period of peace, Russia's errors will no longer be spreading in the United States of America. No longer will Russia be the chosen instrument of God to punish the whole world.

As you read the newspapers, read the fine print. It is reported that Russia is going to reduce its nuclear weaponry from 27,000 to 4,000 by the year 2005. What that really means is they've only got a dozen bombs to drop on Los Angeles instead of 50. Big deal.

Crisis in the Church

The last time I talked in a church the priest demanded that my faculties be removed. Why? Because I gave the pure and simple Fatima Message. I did happen to point out that the Fatima Message is aimed at both individuals and the community. In the United States of America, they worship community. It's a holy word. The truth, however, is that the community is an abstraction, it is a set of individuals who share a common property, mathematically speaking. The community is an abstraction, think about it. It is not a reality. If I go to Hell for ever and ever and you to Heaven, your Heaven won't be one bit less because I am in Hell. If I go to Heaven for ever and ever and you go to Hell, my Heaven won't be one bit less because you are in Hell. That is the absolute God-given truth.

Many of us have abandoned the truth in order to be "politically correct", or for what will get us ahead politically. Jesus said "When the Son of Man returns, will He find any Faith left on this earth?" We are now in a crisis of Faith. Cardinal Ratzinger, after he read the Third Secret, described the Church in one word "crisis".

Fatima and the Bible

Sister Lucy refers to Chapters 8 to 13 in the book of the Apocalypse. Chapter 12 describes Mary's remnant. If you read it closely, it comes down to this: those who are Mary's remnant, those who are under the Blessed Virgin Mary's protection, they are the ones who seek the truth, who love the truth, who believe in the truth and who witness to the truth even unto death. In his conference to bishops, Cardinal Ratzinger says "be ready to be martyrs for the Faith". That is the Blessed Virgin Mary's remnant. It all fits together.

The Fatima Message isn't at odds with the Bible, although the liberals in the Church have diluted everything. Our liberal scripture scholars, who hold sway in the United States, have trashed and trivialized God's word. They even get an "imprimatur" for doing it. Some Jesuit scholars have said that 26 communities wrote Matthew. I don't know why they call it the Gospel according to Matthew. They should call it "the Matthian Communities' Gospel". The reason they do this is simple. It makes it possible to pick and choose what they like, which makes everything diluted, and therefore it disappears.

I remember when I was a Jesuit, a scripture scholar would ask "what does it mean when they say 'they were sitting at the gate'"? Everybody thought it was a trick question. But the answer is, they were sitting at the gate. That's what it said and that's what it meant. They were able to pull stunts like this because they were held in so much reverence, but wrong reverence. I call it the cult of the experts. The experts say this, so this must be true.

Sister Lucy said one of the signs of the end-times is that people will be blind and they will think they are right in their blindness. She also said that one of the signs of the end times is that we would reject the light of truth. In parallel, it is written in Romans 1:16-24, that they rejected God, therefore God delivered them up to sin. Not only did they sin, but they couldn't see sin as sin. They preached sin as good, virtue as vice and vice as virtue. That is a perfect description of our day. I call it "The Romans I Curse". That's what it says, unless

27

you've got a liberal scripture scholar translating your Bible.

I was at the Dead Sea a week and a half ago. We had excerpts from all the books of the Old Testament except Esther. These excerpts proved that in a thousand to thirteen-hundred years, there was no substantial change in the Holy Bible. No change, that is, until the present time. Until 1950. This is when the liberal "rats" really came on the scene. They introduced more changes into the Bible from 1950 until the present than there were in 3,000 years.

Our Lady Knows the Power of Devotions

Thanks to Father Gruner and Father Nault, I have just realized how important these last two days have been, and how important it is to establish devotion to the Immaculate Heart of Mary. The real way you meet people is through devotions. I remember my great aunt bringing me to church and praying before the statues. That will be with me all my life until my dying day. Devotions are what affect people, and it is devotion to Her Immaculate Heart that the Blessed Virgin Mary wants established throughout the world. For example, a statue is brought to India and Moslems are converted just because you carry the statue through the streets. Intellectually, it doesn't make sense. But somehow, people are reached, and even Moslems are converted through these devotions and sacramentals which lead to the sacraments.

To be Catholic we have three areas. First you have to believe, *credendi.* Second, you have to have what I call *orandi,* that is you must have the means of prayer, and especially the Mass and sacraments which makes you specifically Catholic. Third, you have the proper government, the linkage with Rome. To be Catholic, to be in the Church, you must have these three things. In America, *credendi* is almost shot completely. How many bishops in the United States would profess *Extra Ecclesiam Nulla Salus?* They'd weasel out of it. Yet, if you don't have Catholic *credendi*, if you don't have Catholic *orandi* and if you don't have Catholic government, you don't have the Catholic Church. This, in turn, affects the four marks of the Roman Catholic Church; One, Holy, Catholic and Apostolic.

So God has a tremendous problem on His hands. He can't let this continue. That is why Father Gruner said that the year 2000 is a crucial time. We can either be part of the curse or part of the blessing. We can either lead the faithful toward the blessing or toward suffering and the curse. That is our great Fatima opportunity.

The world is under a demonic delusion. Three Popes; Pope Pius XII, Pope Paul VI and Pope John Paul II have said that the sin of this generation is the loss of the sense of sin. We're spiritually psychotic. We're spiritually insane. Last year there was a survey in my country, the Bonner survey. It found that 73 percent of those who call themselves Christians in the United States believe there is no such thing as truth. That's how degenerate we've become. We keep getting worse and worse. All of this is perfectly in line with the Fatima Message. Sister Lucy said that a number of members of the upper clergy are the blind leading the blind. They can not see the problem. Fifteen years ago, while speaking to a large assembly, my Archbishop said "Things aren't as bad as Father Trinchard says they are". He was right. They are worse. "When the Son of Man returns, will there be any faith on earth?" In the face of such crisis, your big opportunity is to bring it back, bring back the Faith.

I'm sure most of you are realists. You all believe in reality. In contrast to this, the typical remark in the United States is "Well, one religion is as good as any other". In other words, there is no objective reality. Whatever you think is best is all right. But reality is what you should think, what you should know. It is not just what you believe is right and wrong, but what you should know is right and wrong. Once when the American Bishops visited Rome, one of them, while dining with the Pope, was trying to justify contraception. The bishop said "Well, those people who are unaware of contraception being wrong are certainly all right". The Pope put down his soup spoon and said "Be that as it may, Bishop, those bishops and priests who should have told them will be in Hell for ever and ever". So there is objective truth. This is the gift of Faith, the evidence of the unseen world. This is what we are here to witness.

Prophecy and Proof

One of the criteria for true prophecy is that it is a speaking forth for God. It is a corrective influence where the priestly tradition is passing on the concrete realities of religion. Prophecy is God speaking forth, through somebody into the present. That is a generic definition of prophecy.

Regarding prophecy, Sacred Scripture gives us guidelines. If someone claims to stand up and speak for God, or claims to have a vision, the Bible tells us to test them. Tell them to prove what they say. The Old Testament taught that if the "prophet" can't prove his words, take him out and stone him to death. That way, you get rid of all who are pretending, and a person will think twice before he pretends to be "prophesying" in God's Name.

Fatima is a prophecy that proves itself by many proofs. Just take the major one, the Miracle of the Sun which occurred 75 years ago. Even the secular press reported it. Nobody could doubt it. Any true prophecy will prove itself conclusively.

Another vital aspect in prophecy is it must agree with God's revelation, the Holy Bible and the authentic magisterial teachings of the Roman Catholic Church. Everything you read through the Councils of the Church that are approved by the Pope, all those dogmatic teachings ultimately come from the Bible and always agree with the Holy Bible. Sacred Scripture and Sacred Tradition are the foundation of our Faith, so it must be in line with Scripture.

Fatima is totally biblical. Sister Lucy tells us to read Apocalypse 8 through 13. While reading scripture, don't get caught up in trivial intricacies. We don't know the color of Jesus' hair, don't know exactly when he was born, don't know his height, we don't know all the things that Americans think are so important. When I was in Israel last week, the people kept asking, "Is this the exact place where Jesus was born?" "Is this the exact place where the shepherds received the good news from the angels?" Let's try not to get bogged down into the minutiae. Get the whole Message of Fatima. Read Frère Michel's books, I recommend them tremendously. They are the best, most comprehensive books on Fatima. Read those books, read the Holy Bible, and be open to the Holy Spirit. The Fatima Message is perfectly logical. The Fatima Message is true prophecy. The Church has totally approved the Fatima Message. The only thing we have got to do is disseminate the message to those who don't know it, and teach the correct message to those within that 5 percent who are familiar with the Our Lady's words at Fatima, but understand Her message in a distorted manner.

Chapter 3

A Vision of Hell
(Hell Exists and We Might Go There)

by Father Marcel Nault

Our Lord Jesus Christ came to earth for one reason, to save souls from Hell. Teaching the reality of Hell is the most important and unavoidable duty of the Holy Catholic Church. One of the greatest Fathers of the Church, Saint John Chrysostom, continually taught that Our Lord Jesus Christ preached more often on Hell than on Heaven. Some people say it is better to preach on Heaven. I disagree. Preaching on Hell produces many more true and strong conversions than only preaching on Heaven. Saint Benedict, the founder of the Benedictines, while he was in Rome, was told by the Holy Ghost: "You're going to lose your soul in Rome and go to Hell." He left Rome and he went into the silence and solitude outside the city to meditate on the life of Jesus and the Holy Gospels. Saint Benedict ran away from those numerous occasions of sin of pagan Rome. He prayed. He made sacrifices for himself and sinners. The Holy Ghost spread the word of his holiness. As a result, people came to see, hear and follow Saint Benedict's example and advice. He separated himself from occasions of sin and became holy. Holiness attracts souls.

Why do you think Saint Augustine changed his life? Because of the fear of Hell. I preach often on the tragic reality of Hell. It is a Catholic Dogma priests and bishops don't preach anymore.

Pope Pius IX, who pronounced the two dogmas of the Infallibility of the Pope and the Immaculate Conception and who also issued his famous Syllabus condemning the errors and heresies of the modern world, used to ask preachers to preach more often on the *Four Last Things*, especially on Hell, as he himself did preach. He asked this because *the thought of Hell makes saints.*

The Saints Feared Hell

Here is something very curious, saints are afraid to go to Hell but sinners are not afraid. Saint Francis de Sales, Saint Alphonsus Liguori, Saint Curé of Ars, Saint Teresa of Avila, Saint Theresa of the Infant Jesus, were all afraid to go to Hell. Saint Simon Stock, the Superior General of the Carmel, knew that his monks were afraid to go to Hell. His monks were fasting and saying prayers. They were living in seclusion, cut off from the dangerous world dominated by Satan. Still they were afraid of going to Hell. In 1251, Our Lady of Mount Carmel appeared in Aylesford, England, to Saint Simon Stock. She said, "Do not be afraid anymore, I am giving you a special vestment; all those who will die wearing this vestment will not go to Hell". I wear my Brown Scapular under my vestments and I have another one in my pocket because I never know when people will ask me to preach on Hell or the Brown Scapular.

Mary said to the Dominican priest, Blessed Alain de la Roche, "I will come and save the world through My Rosary and My Scapular." One cannot specialize himself in everything and preach on everything; one must make a choice. I believe that it is the will of Our Lord Jesus that I preach on Hell. A Monsignor, my superior at that time, once told me: "you preach too often on Hell and you scare people". He added: "Marcel, I have never preached on Hell, people don't like it. You scare them." In a very friendly way, the Monsignor told me in his own office: "Marcel, I have never preached on Hell and

I never will preach on Hell, and look at the nice and prestigious position I hold." I kept a long silence, then I looked him in the eyes. "Monsignor," I said, "you are on the road to Hell for all eternity. Monsignor, you preach to please men, instead of preaching to please Christ and save souls from Hell. Monsignor, it is a mortal sin of omission to refuse to preach the Catholic Dogma of Hell". When God sent prophets in the Old Testament it was to remind men "to come back to the truth, to come back to holiness." Jesus came, preached, and sent His Apostles into the world to preach the Holy Gospels. The Serpent came and spread his poison through heresies, so the Lord Jesus decided to send His Beloved Mother, the Queen of Prophets: "Go to earth and destroy heresies". The Fathers of the Church have written that the Mother of God is the hammer of heresies. If you take the time to study with great attention the Message of Our Lady of Fatima, you will notice it is a most tragic and profound message repeating the teaching of the Holy Gospels. The summary of the Message of Fatima is: Hell exists. Hell is eternal and we will all go to Hell if we die in the state of mortal sin. "What is the use to gain the whole world if you lose your soul?" Our Lady has told us that we can be saved through Her two divine Sacramentals of predestination, the Holy Rosary and the Brown Scapular. There is also special emphasis on Devotion to the Immaculate Heart of Mary and Devotion of the Five First Saturdays.

At the first apparition of the Angel of Portugal at the Cabeço, in May 1916, the Angel came to the three children and he showed them how to adore God with two different prayers. "O my God, I believe, I adore, I hope and I love Thee. I ask pardon for those who do not believe, do not adore, do not hope and do not love Thee." The Angel prayed this while prostrating himself on the ground. The Angel has shown the three children that in the order of prayers, first things first. One must first adore God and then pray to the saints. God first, creatures second. The Angel at Fatima has shown men that we must adore and pray to God on our knees. The more a man knows God, the more he humbles himself in front of God, his Creator. The great French Bishop Bossuet said: "Man is really great when he is on his knees. Yes, man is truly great when he is on his knees in front of his Creator and Redeemer, Jesus in the Most Blessed Sacrament." The Angel at Fatima came to teach the three children that our first duty, according to the First Commandment, is to adore God.

At his third apparition at the Cabeço, the Angel of Portugal came with the Chalice in his left hand and the Host in his right hand. The children wondered what was going on. The Angel miraculously left the Chalice and the Holy Host suspended in the air. The Angel prostrated himself on the ground and recited a profound Trinitarian prayer of adoration. "Most Holy Trinity, Father, Son and Holy Ghost, I adore Thee profoundly and I offer Thee the Most Precious Body, Blood, Soul and Divinity of Jesus Christ, present in all the tabernacles of the world, in reparation for the outrages, sacrilege and indifferences by which He is offended, and by the infinite merits of His Most Sacred Heart and through the Immaculate Heart of Mary, I beg the conversion of poor sinners."

God wants us to adore Him on our knees. Do all of us kneel in prayer and adoration of Jesus in the Most Holy Eucharist? We should. When the three wise men came to Bethlehem and entered the stable, they prostrated themselves in front of baby Jesus to adore Him on their knees. We have the example from Scripture and from the Angel at Fatima that God wants us to adore Him on our knees.

The Reinforcement of Catholic Dogma

One year later, on May 13, 1917, the children saw a young woman appear to them. It was Our Lady's first apparition. Lucy asked, "Where do You come from?" She replied, "I am of Heaven." The Catholic dogma of Heaven. The children asked, "Will we go to Heaven?" She replied "Yes, you will." They then asked, "And Maria das Neves, is she in Heaven?" Mary replied, "Yes." "And Amelia?" "She will be in Purgatory until the end of the world." This girl was around 18 years old. A second dogma, Purgatory exists and will end at the end of this world. The Mother of God cannot lie. The Angel at Fatima taught the three children how to adore God the Father, God the Son, and God the Holy Ghost. This is a reinforcement of the dogma of the Most Holy Trinity, the greatest of them all without which Christianity cannot stand. We must adore the three Persons of the Most Holy Trinity.

A Vision of Hell

On Friday, July 13, 1917, Our Lady appeared at Fatima and talked to the three seers. Our Lady never smiled. How could She smile, for it was on this day that She was to show the children the vision of Hell? She said "Pray, pray very much because many souls go to Hell." Our Lady laid down Her hands and suddenly the three children saw a hole in the ground. "That hole," said Lucy, "was like a sea of fire in which we saw the souls in human forms, men and women, burning, shouting, and crying in despair." Lucy said the demons looked like ugly and unknown animals. The children were so terrified that Lucy screamed. She was so afraid that she thought she would die. Mary said to the children, "You have seen

Hell where sinners go when they don't repent." Another Roman Catholic dogma, Hell.

Our Lady said "Each time you say the Rosary, My children, say after each decade, 'O my Jesus, forgive us our sins, save us from the fires of Hell, lead all souls to Heaven, especially those most in need'." Mary came to Fatima as a Prophet of the Most High to save souls from Hell.

The patron of all pastors, Saint Jean Marie Vianney used to preach that the greatest act of charity towards your neighbors is to save their souls from Hell. The second act of charity, according to Saint Jean Vianney, is to deliver souls from Purgatory. One day in his little church, (where, to this day, his body lies incorrupt) a man possessed by a demon approached Saint Jean Vianney and said: "I hate you, I hate you because you stole from my hand 85,000 souls." Your Eminence, Excellencies, priests, when we will come to be judged by Jesus, Jesus will ask us one question. "I made you a priest, a bishop, a cardinal, a pope, how many souls have you saved from Hell?" Saint Francis de Sales, according to statistics, converted and probably saved more than 72,000 heretics. How many souls have you saved? When you read the Fathers of the Church, the Doctors of the Church and the saints, you are struck by one thing; they all preached the holy Gospel of Jesus and the *Four Last Things:* Death, Judgment, Heaven, Hell. They all preached the Catholic dogma of Hell because when we meditate on the abode of the damned, we don't want to go to Hell. As a result, we avoid the occasions of sin and take all the means necessary to become saints and therefore avoid Hell and attain Heaven.

I don't want to criticize bishops, but I must confess this truth. I have thirty years of priesthood. It is sad to say that I have never seen nor heard a bishop, even my bishop, preach the Roman Catholic dogma of Hell. I suppose in your countries and elsewhere they do, but in America, Hell is not preached. One day in a cathedral I said to a bishop, "Your Excellency, you make a nice meditation of the Holy Rosary every night for the radio. This is beautiful. But I must ask, why don't you have your meditation a little shorter and insert after each decade: 'O my Jesus, forgive us our sins. Save us from the fire of Hell. Lead all souls to Heaven, especially those most in need'. Why do you refuse to say that little prayer after each decade, as requested by Our Lady of Fatima on July 13, 1917, after She had shown Hell to the three seers?" The bishop said to me: "Well, people don't like us to preach on Hell, the word Hell makes them scared." We are not there to preach to please the crowd but to save souls from Hell, to prevent them from going to Hell for all eternity. This may not hold true for all bishops, but I have often heard bishops recite the Rosary and omit that merciful prayer to save souls from Hell. I believe that little prayer of Our Lady of Fatima, given to the children on July 13, 1917, is more powerful and more pleasing to God than any kind of meditation, even given by a holy bishop.

You have received your own missions from God, and I believe that Jesus and Our Lady want me to preach on Hell as my mission. So I preach often on Hell. There are many revelations that we can read in the life of privileged souls. Some souls in Hell have been ordered by God to speak in order to help us in our faith. Those souls in Hell said: "We could accept to be in Hell a thousand years. We could accept to be in Hell a million years, if we knew that one day, we would leave Hell." My friends, we must meditate, not only on the fire of Hell, not only on the privation of seeing God, but we must also meditate on the *eternity of Hell*. Meditate seriously in front of the tabernacle on the Roman Catholic dogma of Hell. Dear bishops, you must preach the whole Gospel of Jesus, including the tragic reality of eternal Hell.

Heretical Concept of God's Mercy

I heard a priest at a charismatic conference tell a crowd of about three thousand people and one hundred priests that "God is love, God is mercy and you will see His infinite Mercy at the end of the world, when Jesus will deliver all souls from Hell, even demons." That priest continues to preach and his bishop doesn't take away his faculties for preaching heresies. "Go into the eternal fire", said Jesus. Eternal fire, not temporal fire. With our limited human intelligence we make a little philosophical proposition, God is love, God is Our Father. How can a father, for Heaven's sake, take little Peter and throw him into a burning furnace? It is impossible. It is an insult to God, Who is love. How many times have you heard that? The truth, however, is that *Hell exists. Hell is eternal. And we will all go to Hell if we die in the state of Mortal Sin.* I can go to Hell. You can go to Hell. If any of us die in sin, we will be in Hell for all eternity, burning, weeping, crying in despair. Not for a million years, but for billions and billions and billions of years and beyond, *for all eternity.* In our lifetime, who has never made one mortal sin? Only one mortal sin not repented before you die is enough for Jesus to throw you into Hell.

One of the greatest Fathers of the Church, Patron of all Catholic Preachers, Saint John Chrysostom said: *"Few bishops are saved and many priests are damned".* In gratitude to the Most Holy Trinity, to Our Blessed Mother, I go to confession every week, I recite my fifteen decade Rosary every day as well as my whole breviary, I wear my Holy Crucifix, the Brown

Scapular, and my heavenly Miraculous Medal. I preach the Rosary and the Brown Scapular. I preach to every one who wants to hear eternal truths, *The Four Last Things*. When we were coming from Lisbon to Fatima by bus, I preached on the bus to the lay people, priests and bishops present. I implored them, "Please, when you come to Fatima, why not make an excellent Holy General Confession? Maybe ten years ago, maybe fifteen years ago, you didn't have the courage to confess that sin because you were ashamed. Please, make a holy and complete confession in Fatima before you leave. There are many priests in Fatima that you will never see until you reach Heaven."

I preach to bishops like I preach to everyone because bishops also have a soul to save. And if bishops are truly humble they will also accept the truth, even from an ordinary simple priest. Let us not leave Fatima without making a Holy General Confession.

Your Excellencies, Jesus made us priests. The Lord Jesus has chosen us from among millions of men to make us priests. We have been made priests to offer the Holy Sacrifice of the Mass to the Almighty Father, to pray the breviary every day, and to preach the Gospel of Jesus to save souls from Hell. Nobody is sure to go to Heaven unless they have received a private revelation from God like the Good Thief on the cross or the three seers of Fatima. Why not take all the insurances that Heaven has given us, the Rosary ("devotion to My Rosary is a sure sign of predestination"), the Brown Scapular and the wonderful sacrament of penance. Preach, my dear bishops, like the Fathers of the Church. The first duty of a bishop is to preach, not to administer a diocese. The Church needs to see and hear bishops preaching like the Fathers of the Church.

If only one bishop among you would have come to

Fatima then return to his diocese and on certain occasions preach *The Four Last Things* with the full Message of Fatima, what a great act of Charity it would be. With the help of the Holy Ghost, say to your faithful: "Listen, my brothers in Christ, I am your bishop, I am here to save your souls from Hell. Please listen, accept and meditate on my teaching today. You, too, my dear priests in my diocese, imitate your bishop, *preach on Hell with the authority that Jesus has given you.*" Preach at least one entire sermon on Hell once a year. You would be doing the greatest act of charity of your priesthood, of your episcopate.

As I mentioned earlier, in my thirty years as a priest, I have never heard a bishop preach on Hell. When I want a sermon on Hell, I have to read Saint John Chrysostom, the Fathers of the Church, the Doctors of the Church and canonized preachers. Dear bishops please, preach on Hell like Jesus, Our Lady of Fatima, the Fathers of the Church and the Doctors of the Church and you will save many souls. *Who saves one soul, saves his own soul.* Preaching on Hell is a great act of charity because those that hear you will believe. They will change their lives and make holy confessions.

People sometimes ask me: "Why is it, Father, that the Brown Scapular isn't preached anymore? In the past, we received the Brown Scapular at First Communion, but today there are no more blessings and imposition of the Brown Scapular. Is the Brown Scapular true today as in the past?" Yes, the Brown Scapular is honored to this day: this truth has not changed. On Saturday, October 13, 1917, during the Miracle of the Sun in Fatima, Mary was holding the Brown Scapular. Sister Lucy said: "The Rosary and the Brown Scapular are inseparable".

Why is it then priests never preach on the Brown

Scapular? How can priests preach on the Brown Scapular if they deliberately refuse to preach on Hell? If you never preach on Hell, people won't believe in Hell. What is the use of wearing the Brown Scapular? Jesus said: "If you have faith, you will move mountains." If you have faith, you will convert souls with the grace of God. If you preach on Hell with faith, people will believe in Hell. Saint Paul said to his disciples: *"Preach with conviction."* To talk or read a homily in a church is not preaching. Preaching is intended to move the will; preaching is intended to move men, to change their lives, to save their souls from Hell.

There are four major reasons why 75,000 priests have left the priesthood:

1) because they have neglected to pray every day.
2) because they did not avoid the occasions of sin and have forgotten that prudence is the science of saints.
3) because they did not have the humility and courage to make holy and complete confessions. Jesus said: "Without Me you can do nothing."
4) because they lived in mortal sin and continued to celebrate thus. If a priest is in the state of mortal sin and celebrates Mass, it is a sacrilegious Mass for him. When he receives Communion, it is another sacrilegious communion for him.

How can a priest in the state of mortal sin preach under the inspiration and the strength of the Holy Ghost? How can he preach if he's filled with demons? Priests, go and make holy confessions and you will become excellent preachers. The Holy Ghost will speak in you and through you and you will save thousands of souls from Hell.

One day, the Curé of Ars received a visit from a young priest from a nearby parish. That young priest was a little curious to meet the Curé of Ars. After lunch the Curé of Ars said: "Will you, please, hear my confession?" The young priest nearly fell off his chair when asked to hear the confession of the already very holy priest, Saint Jean Vianney. *Saints go to Confession! And those that go to Confession become Saints.*

I thank you very much for coming to encourage Father Gruner in making the full Message of Fatima known to the entire world. Father Gruner is a friend of mine and I think he is the man that I love the most on earth. Not as much for his person but because of what he is doing for Our Lady of Fatima: To preach the Message of Fatima and to save many souls from Hell. Dear friends in Jesus and Mary, let us all be true apostles of Our Lady of Fatima.

Before you leave Fatima, I would also like to give you the Brown Scapular. I repeat that Our Lady of Mount Carmel told Saint Simon Stock "Whoever dies wearing the Brown Scapular shall not see the fire of Hell." Read books on Fatima, especially: *The Memoirs of Sister Lucy* and *World Enslavement or Peace: It's up to the Pope* by Father Nicholas Gruner. By the Grace of God, you too will have the courage to preach Fatima's full Message.

Finally, Our Lady of Fatima said: "Pray, pray very much and make many sacrifices for many souls go into Hell because there is no one to pray and make sacrifices." Let us pray often and every day: "O my Jesus, forgive us our sins. Save us from the fire of Hell. Lead all souls to Heaven, especially those most in need."

Chapter 4

In the Grip of the Godless

by Josyp Terelya

I will briefly tell you about my family. I came from a family of high-ranking Communist officials. My father was a cabinet minister. He was a member of the Central Committee of the Communist Party. He was in charge of the KGB, which is the Soviet agents outside of Russia.

My mother completed her schooling at the School of the Central Committee of the Communist Party. She was responsible for atheistic and anti-religious policies in the trans-Carpathian region of Ukraine. I did not live at home. I was raised by my grandmother, and until I was 12, I did not even know of my parents. After the death of my grandmother, my parents took me to live with them. I was 16 years old at the time. I was raised in a religious way, and when I was taken to live with my parents, my brothers and sisters were being raised in a Communist system. My mother raised me in the same fashion. She wanted to change the ways of my upbringing, and conflicts began to appear. I completed college where I studied construction, and then entered the university in Kiev. I was fairly active in the Church of the Catacombs. At 18 years old, I was the leader of the youth wing of the Church of the Catacombs. Here in the West, few know and understand our Church. You know only what you're told in the newspapers. It must not be forgotten that in the Soviet Union, any denomination of any religion was persecuted. In 1946, all of our bishops, including our Metropolitan, were arrested. Thousands and thousands of priests and monks were arrested. All were shot, with the exception of Metropolitan Josyf

Slipyj, Bishop Valescowski, and Bishop Charneski who died in exile. The Church was left without leadership. The people began to organize themselves. For 120 villages we had one priest who would hide in the mountains. The KGB were looking for him. In 1953 he was found and executed. He was shot. Only now, in these times of Perestroika, a few months ago, one of the high-ranking officials in the police, before his death, told where this priest was buried.

Many times the West wrote about me saying I was a fanatic. This is the same thing the Communists would declare. I have been living outside the borders of the Soviet Union for five years, and I see that people are losing their Faith. We cannot say this is only due to our materialistic needs in the modern world. The people themselves are to blame.

Masonry Controls Communism

In the West, very few people know that almost the entire upper echelon of the Communist Party of the Soviet Union were members of the Masonic Lodges. My father was a Grand Master. He accepted membership into the Lodge from Marshal Tito, Khrushchev and Brezhnev. For all intents and purposes, my father controlled all Masonic activity of the lodges in the eastern part of Central Europe. Therefore, many people were astonished when there was discussion about my being freed since President Mitterand, Queen Beatrice and President Reagan took an interest in my being released. I was freed from the concentration camp in 1987. I was stripped of my citizenship and forced to leave the Soviet Union, notwithstanding the fact that the Ukraine has proclaimed so-called independence. I still cannot return to the Ukraine.

During my stay here, I have passed on a multitude of information to the Western governments about what really and truly is happening in the Soviet Union. I obtain my information because I have very close contacts.

When I first came here, I was fairly naive. I thought that everyone in the West was truly against Communism. With time I came to realize that it did not sit well with many members of various Western governments when I did not speak highly about Communists. Many people do not realize the situation of what is happening there. Who created this situation? Why did all the Communists simultaneously denounce Communist Doctrine? The answer is not straightforward. We are witnesses of the fact that more and more people are distancing themselves from God. Satan is working to steal people from God.

In the West I have had the opportunity to speak with many members of the media. They asked me, "how on earth did you survive 23 years of concentration camps and prisons?" I answered, "prayer". They do not understand me. The journalists demand that I tell them how I was tortured and how I was beaten. They need sensationalism. I tell you truthfully that they would beat us and deprive us of food, yet these things would not scare us. A person who prays can be free, with God, even in prison. I was detained in a solitary confinement cell for a period of 7 years. They would give us 300 grams of broth, 4 grams of fat and 22 grams of meat. Yet, as you can see, I am standing here in front of you. I am alive. I made a Rosary out of bread and I considered myself lucky when I had a chance to pray, because if you were caught praying you would be punished. We had to hide our little crosses and Rosaries made of bread because for this you could be severely beaten.

Everyone knew that I was the son of a cabinet minister, everyone knew who my parents were. I was in a special prison where they kept foreigners. There I had the opportunity to meet American officers who were imprisoned during the Vietnam War and being detained even to this day. When I presented this information to the Congress of the United States, I was told that the public does not need to know this. So I kept silent until eleven months ago, when I gave this information to the media.

The Conversion of a Prison Guard

I would like to describe what the surroundings are like to pray in such an environment of extremity. I must explain that in a Soviet concentration camp there were Christians who denounced their faith, who said that God does not exist. These were set free. This was called re-education. However, there were very few Christians who would deny their belief in God. There is one episode where they had beaten me and put me into a small cell made of cement. When I regained consciousness I began to pray for the officer that had beaten me. I prayed out loud. He could not stand it, so he opened the window in the door to the cell and started to yell at me: "Terelya, we will beat you again. I'm an atheist. I don't believe in God and if there is really a God, why isn't He helping you? We can do with you as we please". I continued to pray for him. After a certain time, he again opened the window. This time he wasn't yelling, but he calmly began to converse with me. He said "Josyp, what are you sitting here for? We all know that you are not to blame. Just say that there is no God and they will set you free." I answered that God does not go and beat with a stick. I said that God loves me just as much as He loves you. I said that you have told me that there is no

48

God, you yelled at me and you beat me, and now you are very calmly conversing with me. Is this not God's strength and will? Is this not an act of God? He said, "Fanatic". He closed the window and left. I continued to pray for him. This was already in the evening. He opened the door even though he was not allowed to open the door by himself. He removed from his shoulders a warm overcoat and gave it to me, and he gave me some hot water. The fact of the matter is that in Soviet prison camps they gave 3 cups of hot water one day and cold water the next day. That day I had cold water, and he gave me warm water so I could warm up. He told me, "Josyp, tell me who is Christ?" We spoke into the early morning. I was in that concentration camp for one month. Every time that he would come for his shift he would speak with me. They transferred me to another concentration camp, but that person quit his job with the MPD. He was baptized and became a Catholic. A year later he was arrested. He spent 19 years in the concentration camps. He was recently freed.

The Primacy of Catholic Dogma

A few days ago I was at a conference in Halifax. People ask me "Mr. Terelya, where is it best for us to go, to Fatima, to Lourdes, to one of the others?" I tell them "You can go wherever you wish, whichever suits you financially. But if you do not travel to Fatima or Lourdes, does that mean you will not be Catholics? Do you not believe that wherever two of you meet in the Name of Jesus, that Jesus will be with you?" We should love our Church. We should pray first and foremost in our own churches. We should be active in the daily Catholic life. Then we can go to where we wish. Oftentimes people do not understand this and they say "Mr. Terelya, are you against the apparitions?" No, an apparition is an apparition. An apparition may be recognized by the Church, but the Church has its own doctrine. We're not Catholics simply due to the fact that we were at a certain apparition site. I've seen a type of passivity result from this. At conferences people pray, they pray the Rosary. However when they leave and go to their homes they do not continue this. We should be Catholics daily, not just at the times of conferences. In Halifax I posed this question to 5,000 people at the conference: "Who here prays every night together with their children?" Only 30 hands were raised, and unfortunately, these are people who complain about the priests in their parishes. They complain that their priests do not know how to work with children. The basis of all Christian teaching is given in the home from the mother and father, and then from the priests and the Church. I asked those present, "Who reads the Bible on a daily basis?" Only one hand was raised. This is horrible. We are passive. We are apathetic. We do not take action. How do we explain that in these times we have had the apparitions of Our Holy Mother in the Ukraine and in other places? This tells us that the world is in sin. This speaks of our passivity. This tells us that the Catholic world is becoming passive and atheism is creeping up on us more and more. I am often asked about the new ecumenical movement. I understand ecumenism in only one sense. If a person has welcomed Christ the King to himself and he is a Catholic, then this is ecumenism. Ecumenism can only be Catholic.

We should understand that the foundation of our Catholic Faith is based on Catholic Dogma. We cannot deviate from our Dogma. Why did we survive the catacombs? In 1946 four and a half million Ukrainian Catholics joined the Church of the Catacombs. In 1988, fourteen million Catholics emerged from the catacombs of a totalitarian, Communist country. Where did they come from? Is this not a miracle? Prayer and our Faith is what allowed us to survive and expand. I am convinced that many people do not know the power of prayer. When I recently travelled through the Philippines, I was envious of their relationship and attitude to their faith and the Church. I have seen such deep faith only in our villages, deep in our Carpathian Mountains. Indeed we must really and truly love God and we must want to obey and be faithful to Him.

Our government in Toronto, Canada, has proclaimed that Sunday is now a working day. They have now taken Sunday away from us. Our Blessed Mother says to us "celebrate Holy Sunday". Christians cannot ignore Sunday because Jesus Christ resurrected on Sunday. This is our fundamental feast. Back home in Toronto we have many groups who join together to say the Rosary. Fifty percent of these groups are Philippine. It is very difficult in these times to be a good Christian. Every bishop knows what kind of problems he has. These very large problems include education, the TV, the press, the radio, etc. Today's society does not support Catholicism, and in these extreme times, the Blessed Mother comes to us.

Our Lady Visits the Ukraine

In 1986 there was such a situation in the Ukraine where we felt we would be devastated by the authorities. They were preparing for this, the newspapers were writing it openly. There was an explosion at the Chernobyl Electrical Nuclear Station. Pessimism was at an all-time high. People were very scared. One year after the explosion, the Blessed Mother appeared in Hrushiv. Hundreds and hundreds of people under the rule of the Communists would come there to pray. This was very serious for Moscow. Jews, Russians, the Orthodox and the Moslems all came to Hrushiv. One had to be there to see it in order to believe it. It is difficult to describe in words, one had to live it psychologically. I witnessed 52 Jewish families receiving Christ when a bishop was baptizing them. In one day 3,000 Russians became Catholics. Here in the West, Russians are often thought to be bad people. This is not so. The Russian nation is not a bad nation. The Russian nation is one that has been beaten and martyred. Their government is bad, but the nation itself has been looking for God and has suffered like we did in the Ukraine. When I speak in this manner, the nationalists do not like it.

Moscow Rejects Our Lady of Fatima

One year ago a special group was formed in Washington that travelled from Washington to the Soviet Union. This group was led by John Schepp, a Lutheran minister, as an assistant to President Bush. Catholics travelled with them also. They took Our Lady of Fatima with them to Moscow. When the plane arrived in Moscow, they did not let anyone leave the plane and all on board were detained for 4-1/2 hours. No one was allowed off. They were not welcome. The plane was then forced back to Warsaw. It's one thing to accept money from the West, but it is another thing to accept the Blessed Mother of Fatima in Moscow. These are strictly spiritual interactions and Moscow does not take them lightly.

This year a new group was formed from the United States and Canadian governments. The group from the States was accompanied by Archbishop Hannan of Louisiana. They also took with them the Blessed Mother of Fatima. This was in the year 1992 — five years since the beginning of Perestroika. Russia may be full of wonderful words but they still did not accept the

Blessed Mother of Fatima. She was left in Kiev, Ukraine. This is not a simple matter with Russia. We are still working with the previous personnel of the previous regimes, the same people that my father put to work, and they all worked for the KGB.

Is Russia ready to receive the Consecration? The nation wants it but the government does not. We should not forget that the Russian nation is manipulated by various forces. Five thousand Russian officers have been moved to fight in Serbia. A special school has been formed in the Ukraine where 1,200 Iraqi officers are being trained. The Russian Orthodox Church has begun to purge its ranks of priests and bishops that are not Russian. Some have been killed.

The Rise of Neo-paganism in Russia

Neo-paganism is growing in Russia. Today 70% of the Russian Army are neo-pagans. They are the ones that are calling for a military overthrow. This is why it is so important for the Consecration of Russia to Our Holy Mother's Immaculate Heart. The return to neo-paganism is not simply a fight against Christianity. It is a call for a total massacre of all the Jews in the Soviet Union and a new war. Twenty-two Russian newspapers are calling for this massacre and the Western press is silent about this news. We Christians should not commit sin through our silence. We should speak the truth. Jesus Himself was the Truth and that is why He was so hated. People are taking this matter very lightly; however, we should take it quite seriously. In my short address I cannot touch on all subjects. I have just raised certain fundamental questions that are currently happening in the Soviet Union. In the face of what I have said, the Church has a duty to prevent this war from starting. The Church has a lot of power if it is directed in the right direction.

During a Peace March in Yugoslavia, I saw Muslim villages where the Serbs had butchered the Muslims. Twenty-one kilometers from the city of Mostar, in a very small Muslim village of 65 homes, all the buildings were destroyed and all the people, old and young, were killed. I was witness to them cutting off hands, the breasts of women were cut off, eyes were poked out. This is not just a national war between the Serbs and the Croatians. This is something greater. This is a manifestation of total hatred. This is the work of satan. People are God's creation, and we are witnessing satan attempting to destroy God's creation. He is destroying people, destroying them in a very brutal fashion in the 20th century. Some people say that I live very far from this, why do I care? No, we should become involved and speak out about this. We should pray more because it may be too late.

Following the Peace March in Yugoslavia, Moscow allowed me to hold a similar Peace March in Hrushiv. On June 26, I travelled from Vienna to Czechoslovakia in order to travel to the Ukraine. On the 26th I was illegally arrested by the Czech KGB. I was held in prison for three days in Bratislava, and I was returned back to Austria. Over the three days I was not given any food or water. I was beaten and parts of me are still blue. A week later I illegally crossed the border and I was arrested in Hungary. Although the Hungarians arrested me, they treated me well. The officers of the Hungarian KGB were asking me for my autograph. They told me "Josyp, we have to return you back because you are here illegally".

On August 24, there was a large gathering in Hrushiv. There were 370,000 Catholics attending including 40,000 Orthodox. We had a procession. This is the first time in our history that the Orthodox have come together for this retreat with the Catholics.

Moscow Prevents Consecration by Threatening Vatican

Many times during conferences I am questioned on very delicate topics which I cannot answer. I have a lot of information. I oftentimes meet with His Holiness the Pope. The Holy Father cannot do everything that he wishes to do, because Moscow has been giving the Vatican specific obligations to meet. Many people complain that the Consecration of Russia has not yet taken place. We must not forget that in the Soviet Union there are approximately 22 million Catholics, and not just the 14 million Ukrainian Catholics, which the orthodox Church and the Church of Moscow will not tolerate. It was our Church that raised the people's awareness to their freedom and independence, and we should unite all the Catholic interests, all of the Catholics in the Soviet bloc.

There are 1,015,000 Russian troops in the Ukraine. Ukraine does not have its own borders. Everything is under the control of Moscow. The Russian papers are saying that "if you demand more freedom, then we will blow up a few more nuclear electrical generating stations and you will be like the Dead Sea." We are in a very delicate situation, the same way that Catholicism is in the entire Soviet Union. Officially, they have given us the right to pray and have opened the churches, but the governmental decree for the rehabilitation and legalization of our Church has not been made.

Regarding the Vatican-Moscow Agreement, I had a seven-hour discussion with Cardinal Ratzinger, Cardinal Silvestrini and Cardinal Willebrands. For seven hours we spoke and Cardinal Willebrands said, "why did Ostpolitic happen?" It happened because the Vatican felt that they might be able to include the hierarchy of the Russian Orthodox Church into theirs. That is what they thought. He even said that "this was our biggest downfall because we thought that way". And now it is very difficult to rework all the old politics.

I received a letter from Cardinal Casaroli in which the topic of the Consecration has been discussed. Many Bishops and Cardinals and many Faithful in Saint Peter's Square are willing to do this but they are waiting for the proper timing. This is a private letter and my conscience will not allow me to release the contents because no one has given me permission to do so. However, I can say that this is a very complex question. You must remember that Moscow is putting great pressure on the Vatican not to do the consecration. They are warning the Vatican that if they in fact do this, then they will devastate the Catholics in their territory. This is a very delicate item. It depends on the bishops as well as the Faithful.

Part II
The Window of Opportunity

Chapter 1

The Window of the Present

by Father Nicholas Gruner

I think that because of the actions of His Holiness, Pope John Paul II, and those few bishops who joined His Holiness in consecrating the world, we have a special window of opportunity today in 1992. When the Pope consecrated the world in 1982, and again in 1984, a grace was given which we are realizing today. But it is not exactly the grace as it is often interpreted. The grace is not the conversion of Russia, not just yet. The grace is, rather, the window of opportunity. Between 1929 and 1992 there have been only a few windows of opportunity where it would have been very easy for the bishops and the Pope to consecrate Russia.

A few years ago, Mr. Gorbachev apologized in public to the proletariat of the world for the excesses of the Communist regime. Therefore, to make an act of consecration and reparation should not be, nor could it be construed today as, an affront to the Communist Regime. If the President, the head of state himself, made this act of apology to the proletariat of the world, then it could not be construed as an insult for the Pope to make an apology to God for the excesses of the Communist Revolution.

However, I believe this opportunity will not last forever. It could be, perhaps, the last one before the blood bath. That's an opinion. I could be wrong. I am not a prophet. I do not know the future. But there have been six Glasnosts and six Perestroikas since 1917. This is the sixth one. After each one there has always been a hardening and always been a reverse. Lenin had the first one with his economic policy. Stalin had his five-year plan. Each time, they said — "we went too far. We want to go back to the free market economy" — they said whatever the West wanted to hear. Stalin had a second one at the beginning of the Second World War in order to have the co-operation of the Russian people themselves. When the German armies came into Russia at the beginning of the war, the Russians welcomed them with open arms. Obviously Stalin did not have the loyalty and support of the small people. In order to reverse this, he went back to another Glasnost and Perestroika. There was an opening up again to religion, even to liberty for religious practice, in order for the Russian people to save mother Russia.

We have had peaceful co-existence since 1965. We have had detente since 1970 and now we have Perestroika. It has always been the same tactic, two steps forward one step back. But it is a tactical maneuver. The goal is the same. We are, right now, at a moment when the leaders of the Russian Revolution and their successors, whatever you wish to call them today, would find it difficult to take offense for such an apology given to God when the President of the Republic himself did the same thing.

So this is especially a grace. I do not wish to minimize or appear to minimize the great good work that Pope John Paul has done in the Act of Consecration of 1984. All the same I insist, as the Pope himself has said, and as Sister Lucy has said, this 1984 consecration of the world "is not the 'Consecration' that was requested at Fatima." But, as I wrote at the time, in 1984, it is still a grace. We see the fruits of this grace but that will not go on forever. That's why I am very concerned that the Church, especially the bishops and the Pope, should seize this opportunity in the near future. These periods do not last long. At the most, I expect, it will be one or two years before the door will close, the hardening will come, and the rhetoric and the propaganda will be different. Russia is like Germany was before the Second World War, that is — it is economically destitute. The only difference between Russia and Germany is that Germany did not have at the beginning of its destitution the military might that Russia has today and can use immediately. They do not have the economic wealth to feed their people because they are putting more than 40% of their gross national product into the military even to this day. Therefore, when it becomes politically necessary, they will have to change their propaganda. It will take something to maintain an economic balance: keep the war machine going. I don't make a study of military technicians but one of the most brilliant in our time is Marshall Ogarkov. He wrote that "Plan B for 1982" was to have been an unprovoked, sudden, all out nuclear attack on the United States. This is published. This is not my own invention. He published it in 1982 whereby he estimated that the United States would lose 135 million people in the first half-hour of war. It was to be an unprovoked attack and it was to be totally sudden.

Many people don't realize that such an attack was on its way two years later, but the Russians mysteriously lost their most important force on Our Lady's feast day, May 13, 1984. Half of it mysteriously blew up and it took them two years to reconstruct that stockpile in the Kola Peninsula just north of Norway. The NATO observers watching the USSR Navy break out were not only amazed and frightened, they were terrified. There was nothing they could do to stop it.

When an Opportunity is Seized

It was on May 13, 1955, that the Russian armies withdrew from Austria. They had occupied Austria for ten years. It was during this occupation that a certain Father Peter led a Rosary campaign in Austria and had 10% of the population involved. Theresa Neumann, the stigmatist of Austria, said that it was definitely the Rosaries of the people that accomplished it. Ten percent of the people were praying the Rosary every day, as they pledged to do. The Russian diplomats had refused to withdraw from Austria even though the Allies (the United States, England and France) wanted them to leave. Russia said "No. We want to stay." But they reversed themselves. It was May 13, 1955. Napolean himself said, "He who wishes to control Europe, must control Austria." So, in spite of the tactical advantage, despite their will not to leave, Austria was delivered because 10% of the Austrian people prayed the Rosary.

Sister Lucy has said of the Rosary, "There is no problem, national or international, either moral or physical that cannot be solved by the Rosary." She says, in fact, that, "In our time, because of the increasing power of evil, God has given increased power to the Rosary." You will find her statement, made to Father Fuentes in 1957, in Frère Michel's book. In fact there is an entire chapter just on that interview. It is an authentic statement of Sister Lucy made to Father Fuentes at that time, in spite of what commentaries may have been made about it.

Assuming Responsibility

It is important to keep our perspective. We must never forget that Our Lady did promise the Triumph, that She will win. Father Joseph de Sainte Marie, a Carmelite theologian who was a professor at the Pontifical Faculty of the Teresianum, wrote some brilliant works on Fatima which we have published. In fact, in my book, *World Enslavement or Peace*, we have, with his permission, the whole of his "Reflections." It is about forty pages of smaller print. (I think he was less than fifty years old when he died in 1985.) He points out that Our Lady uses the words, "in the end", or, in Portuguese it might be, "finally", or, as in Italian, "finalmente", indicating, as he says, that there is a problem to overcome first.

I think we must realize that from the beginning there has not been enough reflection on the fact that the children, in a sense, because they accepted responsibility, died a martyr's death. It is actually more precise to say that they had a dry martyrdom. They were threatened with death on August 13 by the Mayor of Ourem, a town about ten miles from Fatima. They were threatened because they would not deny seeing the beautiful Lady from Heaven. They would not reveal the Secret until Our Lady let them. They were being ordered to destroy their credibility by either denying what they had said before, or alternatively, showing themselves not to be trustworthy by revealing the Secret that Our Lady told them to keep for a time. If they did not do so, the mayor told them he would boil them in oil.

Now, I reflect on this because the Message of Fatima and the fulfillment of this message means the defeat of Satan *finalmente*. Sister Lucy has said, "The Blessed Virgin did not tell me this but She made me understand that we are in the final battle between satan and the Blessed Virgin." Reflecting on this very point she noted that, in a final battle, there is one winner and one loser. And the devil is spoiling for his final battle. This will give you some sense of the drama we are all living at this very moment. We are asked to participate in it. To do our part.

I remember speaking to Monsignor Pio Abresch. He is in the Congregation of the Bishops in Rome. Padre Pio said of him that he would go high in the Vatican. Just before I was ordained I went to see him. He said, "Do you know what Padre Pio said to me before I was ordained? He said, 'if you knew the responsibility that you were assuming by becoming a priest, you would not accept it.'" It would seem that Monsignor Abresch was trying to tell me the same thing. I pass this on to you because, the fact is, by becoming bishops you have assumed a responsibility for the Message of Fatima even if you have never heard of Fatima, by the very fact of accepting the charge of the bishop's office. That is why our prayers have been with you for months and years even though we have not met you before, because we know of the heavy responsibility you have. We also know it is impossible for you, as it would be impossible for me, or anyone else, to carry it out without the grace of God. That is why when we speak of the Fatima Message, we are trying to tell the truth as plainly as we know, without exaggeration, but at the same time without diminution either. It is not a question of us being better or holier. But I would do wrong to hide the truth from you if I came here to tell you the Message of Fatima and then hid it from you in order to make you feel good.

The Consequences of Delay

Often the accusation is made, "But Father Gruner is against the Holy Father." We are not against the Holy Father. We have never been against the Holy Father. We have published time and time again that we are among his most loyal sons. Loyal not only to him but to each one of you, the bishops.

But I take literally the words, "Make it known to My ministers", that Our Lord spoke to Lucy. First of all, it is a duty, a duty that we cannot avoid even though it is unpleasant. But Our Lord says, "Make it known to My ministers." In other words, He does not want us to hide it. Secondly, he wants the consequences of ignoring the Message of Fatima to be known. Those consequences are horrendous. The King of France had his head chopped off for not obeying the command given through St. Margaret Mary, and he was a very holy man. He is considered one of the Holy Monarchs of France. I believe that his cause, the cause of Louis XVI, has been introduced. Yet, because he delayed and because his two predecessors had delayed for one hundred years, he paid the price, both for himself and for his predecessors. He tried before he was beheaded to consecrate France to the Sacred Heart as Our Lord had commanded it to be done by Louis XIV but the problem was, he was in prison. He could not do it with the appropriate, public solemnity necessary.

I have wondered what Our Lord means by "delay". There are different ways of delaying. There is, of course, a delay simply by just not doing something when we have been told to do it. This is, shall we say, a negative delay. We just don't do anything. There is also a positive delay, which is to actually impede others from fulfilling this command. Now just exactly to whom is Our Lord referring when He says, "Make it known to My ministers that they follow the example of the King of France in delaying the execution of My command and like him they will follow him into misfortune"? He does use the word 'ministers' in the plural. That is part of the patrimony of Fatima. It is something that you can read independently of anything I have published. You can read Sister Lucy's *Memoirs* all in her own handwriting. This part is also carried in her book *Memõrias E Cartas da Irma Lucia*, published in Porto in 1972 and again in 1976. There are a few extra documents in the 1976 edition.

We are all in a very difficult position. All of us, lay people, priests, bishops and the Holy Father, as well as the non-believing will suffer terribly in what will happen if we do not have this consecration in time.

Proven Consequences

Had the consecration been done in 1929, we would not have had the Second World War, Our Lady makes it very clear. On July 13, 1917, She said, "If mankind does not amend, then God will punish the world by means of war, hunger, persecution of the Church and persecution of the Holy Father. To prevent this I shall come to ask for the Communions of reparation on the First Saturdays and for the consecration of Russia." She went on to say, "When you see a night illumined by an unknown light, know that it is the great sign that God is about to punish the world" (by these four punishments). That great sign was seen on January 25, 1938, the feast, very significantly, of the Conversion of St. Paul. It was seen all over Europe by tens of millions of people. People in Switzerland, at 11:00 at night, could read their newspapers by this strange light.

It was a special kind of red like that, nuclear scientists say, which is seen after a nuclear blast. It was seen in North America as a white light. I spoke with a priest who was a seminarian in Austria at the time and he said the sky was so red that the chaplains in the seminary did not have Benediction that night because they thought there was a great fire in the city somewhere and they were waiting for a phone call for them to go out to assist the dying. Only afterwards, one professor told him in the privacy of his room, "This is the sign of Our Lady of Fatima."

Now, when Sister Lucy saw this on January 25 (it extended into the morning of January 26, until 3:00 a.m., or thereabouts), she cried because she knew the Second World War was about to begin. Forty-five days later Hitler invaded Austria. This occurred during the reign of Pope Pius XI as Our Lady had predicted. Now, at the time when Our Lady said this, the reigning pope was Pope Benedict XV. Sister Lucy was told that it would be in the reign of Pius XI that the war would begin and that this sign would precede it. There, then, are three prophecies, all of which were realized within twenty-one years of Our Lady's appearance in 1917. In that very same year the "errors of Russia" were on the rise, even though people could not believe Russia was a threat. It was one of the weakest of countries because of the civil war it had suffered and because the First World War had just been endured. Russia appeared a threat to nobody in 1917. Yet Our Lady spoke of Russia.

There is Only One Fatima

Some people think that because we believe in Fatima, we are simpletons. That because we believe in the full Message of Fatima, we are really not intelligent enough, that we don't know what is going on in the world. Let us leave them in their ignorance, we don't want to disturb their peace. This is how the Modernists work. What the Modernists have done to Isaiah is what they have done to the Message of Fatima. They say, Part One, up to 1917, that is true. But Part Two, what took place in 1925 and 1929, Sister Lucy, though she is a very nice lady, very pious, very holy, she invented it.

There is no Part One! There is no Part Two! There is only one Fatima! This theory that there is a Fatima One and a Fatima Two has poisoned the minds of even good theologians, those whom we, in North America, would call Conservative, Orthodox or Traditional. They have been poisoned by this theory not even realizing its source. That is why Frère Michel, in his first volume, *The Whole Truth About Fatima*, spent 150 pages of the English edition not only disproving this theory but demonstrating the dishonesty of its unique and only author, the Belgian Jesuit, Father Dhanis. Dhanis wrote this theory in 1944. Frère Michel says that in 1944 Dhanis could be excused from holding such a theory because of the distortions that pious authors had made in the second part of the Secret. For example, in order not to disturb the Allies, the word "Russia" was removed even though it was clearly in Sister Lucy's writings, and replaced with "the forces of evil" or some such phrase. Therefore, it was easy to see that there had been tampering with the text. Father Dhanis could detect that something was altered. Also, during the war there was not as much opportunity for communication as there was after the war. Dhanis did not have the opportunity to consult the documents or to consult with Sister Lucy or to consult with her confessors. That, of course, changed after 1945 and Father Dhanis was offered the opportunity to speak with her, to look at the original documents and to talk with her confessors. Remember now, his theory maintained that Sister Lucy made it up (certain ingredients of the Message) in the light of events of the Second World War and that she never said these things before 1940. But when he was offered a look at the documentation, to speak to the witnesses who could disprove his theory, he refused to talk to them. He refused to be informed. So, whereas before 1945 he could be held to maintain that opinion honestly, but in error, after his refusal, he could no longer be considered an honest theologian.

But it is this theory which, nevertheless, has to this day poisoned the minds of many theologians including some in the Vatican itself. It is because of this theory that some of us are considered simpletons. I don't mind being considered a simpleton because of this false theory but the problem is we are all going toward disaster if this falsehood, which has been perpetrated against Sister Lucy since 1944, is allowed to poison the minds of the bishops and the counselors of the Pope.

I raise this point because many people have not even thought of such an idea. Yet it still poisons the mind, even of those who have never heard of it. The dynamic is similar to the damage done by the writings of Teilhard de Chardin. Today no one reads Teilhard but he still does his damage because he has poisoned the intellectual climate with regards to the true Catholic teaching about creation. Similarly, Father Dhanis has poisoned the intellectual climate of theologians with regard to the full Message of Fatima.

There has been an organized attempt, through politics, through pressure tactics, to silence the full Fatima Message. It concerns Russia. It concerns the events after 1917. The sooner we recognize that this is going on, the better. This is why I very much appreciate that all of you bishops have taken this opportunity at least to hear the other side. We are aware of argumentation of the problems that are raised intellectually. We are prepared to answer them. Our Lord has a very simple answer. He says, for delaying the execution of "My command," ... "My ministers" ... will have their heads chopped off! It is not a very pleasant image. But I think I am being more loyal to the Holy Father and to you bishops by bringing this truth to you than by hiding it from you.

Fatima is a Public, Prophetic Revelation

There is another theory about the Message of Fatima that has poisoned the minds of the bishops and the theologians and the advisors of the Pope. That is the theory that Fatima is a 'private revelation'. Father Joseph de Sainte-Marie and also Bishop Graber have written that there are three kinds of revelations, not two kinds. There is the 'public deposit of Faith' and there is 'private revelation'. But there is also the third kind which is called 'public, prophetic revelation.'

Fatima is treated as if we can have the option of ignoring it without consequences to ourselves. When it comes to Fatima, that theory is false.

Now, I have never seen the Blessed Virgin. If I were to tell you I had seen the Blessed Virgin, that would be a private revelation to me. You, of course, would have no obligation to believe me, but Fatima is not in that category because Fatima has been backed by a miracle and by public prophecy that has been proven time and time again. Our Lord, speaking to the cities of Capharnaum and Bethsaida said, "And thou Capharnaum, and thou Bethsaida, do you think you will go as high as Heaven? No. You shall be cast as low as hell." And why? Because, He says, "if Sodom and Gomorrah had seen the miracles that had been worked in you they might have done penance and stood to this day."

God is just but He is also unequal. I'll explain what I mean. He gave the miracles to Capharnaum and Bethsaida which he did not give to Sodom and Gomorrah. Knowing full well had He given those miracles to Sodom and Gomorrah they might have repented, yet he did not give them those miracles. He gave them to Capharnaum and Bethsaida. They refused the grace that He gave and He said for this reason, and this reason alone, they were going to be cast as low as Hell. So, to refuse a message of God certified by public miracles is obviously a serious matter.

What will Our Lord say to the 20th century? "And thou 20th century, do you think you will be raised as high as Heaven? No. You will be cast as low as Hell because I did not work the Miracle of the Sun before the Pharisees who said to me, 'Show us a sign in the Heavens and we will believe in You.'" But, at the request of Our Lady of Fatima, He did.

Will He say to us then, "Well, you thought it was a private revelation so you're off the hook"? I'm sorry. He expects a little more intelligence from us.

Fatima is a 'public, prophetic revelation'. Father Joseph de Sainte-Marie said, "There is a relationship between the hierarchy and the prophet." It is explained in Scripture, Ephesians 2:20. We are all familiar with the first half of the verse but not with the second half. The Church is "built upon the foundation of the apostles and the prophets, with Christ Jesus, Himself, as the cornerstone". The prophets referred to are the prophets of the New Testament.

St. Thomas Aquinas tells us that God sends prophets to every generation not to give a new doctrine but to remind the faithful of what they must do to save their souls. The Church is founded upon the apostles and the prophets. It is the role of the prophet to deliver the message God gives. It is the role of the apostles to determine if the prophet indeed comes from God. The apostle does not have the option of ignoring it. He must examine it. He does not have the option of saying everything or anyone that comes forward is true. Once examined and found to be true, he is bound to hold onto it himself. We have that in 1 Thessalonians 5: 19 to 22. St. Paul writes, "Do not extinguish the spirit. Do not despise prophecy. Test all things and hold fast to that which is good." If we can just say to any prophetic revelation that God gives that it is just a private revelation that we can ignore if we simply choose to do so, then we are, in effect, despising prophecy. If it is truly just a private revelation we can ignore it with no obligation. No problem. If we do not make this important distinction between private revelations and true public prophetic revelations, we can end up falling into the very crime of despising prophecy and extinguishing the spirit.

Sister Lucy refers to refusing the light of the truth, the known truth. Refusing the known truth is a sin against the Holy Spirit for which there is no forgiveness. She says, "My mission is not to indicate to the world the material punishments which are certain to come if the world does not pray and do penance beforehand. No! My mission is to indicate to everyone the imminent danger we are in, of losing our souls for all eternity if we remain obstinate in sin."

It is since she said this that she has been kept silenced for over thirty years.

A Mother Cannot Be Kept Silent

It is amazing that in 1966, on November 15, Pope Paul VI abrogated Canons 1399 and 2318 of the old code. The new code reflects this change. Those two canons of the code stipulated that to publish about apparitions, whether approved by the Church or not, you needed the *imprimatur* of a bishop. After November 15, 1966, no such permission was necessary. Anyone in the whole Catholic Church can publish anything, attributing the most fantastic statements to Our Lady in some apparition somewhere, without further permission from the Church. The one person who, to this day, is not allowed to speak, yet who is best known, and who knows more about the Message of Fatima than anyone else is Sister Lucy. She is not allowed to speak about anything on Fatima that has not already been published in her Memoirs, without explicit permission of either Cardinal Ratzinger, the head of the Congregation for the Doctrine of the Faith, or the Pope himself. That has been the situation since 1960.

They have tried to explain it as being because she is a Carmelite and enclosed, and therefore not able to speak. But, many of you have Carmelite convents of enclosed nuns in your dioceses and I am sure that you are able to speak to any Sister behind the grill whenever you choose and you do not need permission of the Vatican to do so. But with one nun in the whole Catholic Church that condition is laid down. That is Sister Lucy. In my view, it is a crime. It is a grave injustice, not only to Sister Lucy but much more importantly to the Church, because the Blessed Virgin came with a message for the salvation of souls. This message is intended for the faithful, for the bishops, as well as for the Holy Father.

In 1982 when the Holy Father came to Fatima he made an allusion to the Third Secret. He said, "To understand the Message of Fatima we must understand it is the message of a Mother. It is the key to understanding the whole Message." He said that at the beginning. Then he said, "Can the Mother who, with all the force of love that She fosters in the Holy Spirit, who desires everyone's salvation, remain silent when She sees the very foundation of Her children's salvation undermined?" The Pope answered his own question with, "No. She cannot remain silent."

What is the basis of our salvation? If we turn to Sacred Scripture we find what it is — it is our Faith. Our Lord, speaking in St. John's Gospel, says the first work that is pleasing to Him is to have faith in Him. To take it from dogmatic theology, the creed of St. Athanasius says "Those that wish to be saved, before any good work, must above all hold on to the Catholic Faith, whole and entire." That is the foundation of our salvation. "Without the Catholic Faith", he goes on to say, "you cannot save your soul."

I believe it is also defined in the First Vatican Council. There is no excuse for any Catholic to leave the Catholic Faith. That is with an *anathema sit* attached to it. The Blessed Virgin sees our salvation is undermined. It is undermined from within. She comes to warn us all. It is much more convincing coming from Her than from Father Gruner who is a poor sinner. That is why Sister Lucy should be allowed to speak. That is why the Third Secret should be revealed. They can say I am a bad person or I am against somebody or I don't have this paper or whatever, but they will dare not say that of Her. That is why it is much more important that the words of Our Lady be heard by the Bishops and the Faithful.

I know that if I were a pastor, no Bishop here could give me charge of a parish and then say, "but, Father, you are not allowed to hear confessions; Father, you are not allowed to baptize the members of the Faithful who come to you for baptism." You cannot give me the onus, the *munus,* the duty of the office and then not give me the means to carry out my job. I am only telling you this truth because, similarly, I do not believe the bishop can be given charge of a diocese and at the same time not be given the means to carry out their *munus*, their duty of office.

For this generation the Third Secret is necessary, because we are living it now. You have a right to the truth, not only for your own souls but particularly for the souls that are entrusted to your care. I believe you have a right to ask for the Secret to be given to you. You have been charged with the care of souls, of millions and millions of souls. If the Holy See has enough confidence in your ability to take care of these souls then they have no reason not to let you know the Third Secret. Our Lady, in Her own words, tells you that the Faith is being undermined from within and She cannot remain silent. Yet, She Herself has been silenced for the last thirty years.

We are Living the Third Secret

If the Message of Fatima were known and understood, fully, you would not need this conference. You would know what to do. You would not need me or anyone else to tell you what to do. If you had the full Message of Fatima, you would realize that Our Lady is speaking about the time from 1960 onwards. You would know that we are living the Third Secret. We are living through the Apostasy predicted in Sacred Scripture.

Sister Lucy is so circumspect when it comes to the Bishops and to the Holy Father. In the early 1940's when she was given a message by Heaven to pass on to the bishops of Spain, she would not pass it on because it was very critical of them. Not until she was commanded by her bishop confessor did she do it. Once delivered, it received, at first, the very reception she had expected it to find. Finally it was accepted, respectfully at least.

We can begin to understand why it took Sister Lucy three months of agony to write down the Third Secret. She had no trouble writing down the Second Secret regarding the annihilation of nations. But to write down the 25 lines of the Third Secret, she did agonize for three months even though she had an order of obedience that she wanted to obey. When it came to the Third Secret she agonized, she went through pain, she could not do it, could not put her pen to paper, although she tried as hard as she could. It took an intervention of the Blessed Virgin to tell her, "Yes. Put it on paper."

It can only be as Cardinal Oddi has written and as we published, at his request, in our magazine, *The Fatima Crusader*, that the Third Secret is something terrible.

The Third Secret is something that concerns the hierarchy, particularly the bishops and the Holy Father.

The essence of the Third Secret has two parts. One is the dangers to the Faith. The second is the responsibility of the hierarchy, the bishops, cardinals and the Holy Father. We don't have a copy of the text in front of us but we can know much about the Third Secret from all the circumstances around it. From all the things said by Cardinal Ottaviani, by Cardinal Ratzinger, by Sister Lucy and by the events that surrounded the transmission of the Third Secret.

I challenge anyone to read the Third Volume of Frère Michel's *The Whole Truth About Fatima* trilogy, and tell me they are not convinced they have the substance of the Third Secret. No one can come back and say the substance of the Third Secret has not been proven or, at least, that they do not now have a serious understanding of it.

Frère Michel of the Holy Trinity has based his work largely on the research of Father Alonso, a Claritian Father who was appointed as the archivist of the Fatima Shrine by Bishop Venancio from 1965 until Father Alonso's death in 1981. Father Alonso is a very interesting, a very honest theologian. I met him for a few weeks in 1981, about four months before he died. Father Alonso, in 1965, thought that the Third Secret was unimportant and should remain sealed. By 1976 he had changed his mind and said so publicly. Between 1976 and 1981 he published short articles on the Third Secret in which he said the Third Secret concerned dangers to the Faith. He wrote this at least three years before the same point was published through Cardinal Ratzinger's interview with Vittorio Messori for the 1984 book, *The Ratzinger Report*. Very gingerly, very carefully, he also suggested the second half of the Third Secret refers to the responsibilities of the hierarchy for the apostasy that has invaded the Church today.

Now Sister Lucy has always corrected theories about the Third Secret if they were false or if they were way off base. She has never corrected Father Alonso's theory from the time he published it up to the present day.

There are two Cardinals here today. They have a right to speak to Sister Lucy without permission of the Holy See. I would invite them to find out for themselves while they are here in Fatima. Speak to Sister Lucy and see if she has permission to reveal the Third Secret or to speak authoritatively about many things in the Fatima message.

In 1983 John Haffert and the Blue Army said that the consecration of 1982 had fulfilled the request of Our Lady of Fatima. They claimed Sister Lucy was the author of this statement. Father Joseph de Sainte-Marie wrote to Sister Lucy and asked her to confirm or deny these statements that were widely circulating. She wrote back and said, "I cannot speak about that, I do not have permission of the Holy See." On March 19, 1983, Archbishop Sante Portalupi asked for an interview with Sister Lucy on behalf of the Holy Father. She explained that the Consecration was not done, but she also explained, "I could not say so before because I did not have permission of the Holy See."

The letters that you may have seen are circulated with Sister Lucy's signature on them. According to the expert I hired, they are fake signatures. Others claim them, still, to be true. However, they are obviously false because they contradict known facts that Sister Lucy herself knows about.

Furthermore, in keeping with her role of not speaking about things in public without permission of the Holy See, nowhere in all these letters does she make an allusion to having this permission. Sister Lucy has been silenced. What these so-called experts on Fatima refer to as Fatima One includes the message to say the Rosary, which is, of course, very nice and very holy, and to wear the Scapular, also very nice and very holy, and to keep the Commandments, all things that are very fine. But when they talk about the request for the Consecration of Russia, they accuse Sister Lucy of making it up. They are much more pious about it than that, they say she is either crazy or she is a liar. That is what she is accused of by Father Dhanis and his followers, to this day.

Sister Lucy has not defended herself and has not defended the Message because, in her mind, she has entrusted it to the Church. The ball is in your court, you the bishops. If you do nothing with it, she can still go before God and say "I did what I was told to do." I don't believe the bishops of the Church and the Holy Father can give to God the same answer as can Sister Lucy. She is certainly willing to tell the truth in season and out of season. Time and again when these theories (that the Consecration has been done) have gone abroad, first after 1942, then after 1952, 1964, 1982 and then again 1984, Sister Lucy has always come back, when asked, and when she was able to speak, and said, "No." She has been consistently saying "No" for the last fifty years.

There is a Prophet in Israel

We must understand the role of a prophet, in God's Providence. In the Old Testament, Naaman, the Syrian General, had leprosy. The Jewish maid, helping the wife of Naaman said, "Your husband can go to Israel and be cleansed because there is a man of God there. There is a prophet there." Naaman went with a large retinue and the King of Israel rent his garments and said, "Am I God that I can cure anybody?"

Eliseus sent a message to the king and to Naaman to let them know that there was a prophet in Israel. "Send him to me". Eliseus then sent a message to Naaman. He was told by Eliseus to, "Go down to the River Jordan and bathe there seven times."

Naaman got angry and said, "Do we not have better rivers in Syria than here?" His counsellors prevailed with him and said, "If he had asked you to do something difficult, you would have done it. Do what he says." So Naaman washed himself seven times and his skin became as white, as clean as a baby's, as Sacred Scripture tells us.

There are two points in this story to consider. First of all, an act of obedience is asked for. Not six times, not eight times, not five times, but seven times. Secondly, the king thought somehow or other that Naaman the great general, with his retinue of soldiers, was trying to pick a fight with him, when all Naaman was trying to do was to get himself cleansed from leprosy. Eliseus knowing of this misunderstanding sent a message.

Eliseus said, "Let Israel know that there is a prophet in Israel." He worked this miracle not only for Naaman but also for Israel. Our Lord, speaking of that incident, said there were many lepers in Israel at the time of Naaman but only one was cleansed from his leprosy by the prophet. We have a prophet among us and Lucy, in her humility, will say, "I am not a prophet." But the fact is, theologically speaking, Sister Lucy is a prophet. She has been certified by God, by a public miracle. Not only the Message of Fatima is certified but the messenger has been certified by this miracle. Let the Catholic Church know that there is a prophet in Israel today, in the new Israel of God, the Catholic Church. Let us wake up to realize it before it is too late.

Sister Lucy is 85 years old this year, born March 22, 1907, just two weeks before my mother's birthday; that's why I remember it. There is a prophet in Israel and God has worked a great miracle for us to know that.

Someone says, "Is Lucy more important than the Pope? Does she command the Pope?" Father Joseph de Sainte-Marie explains; "It is the role of the prophet to speak, it is the role of the hierarchy to judge if it comes from God. Once discovering that this message comes from God, then the Holy Father and the bishops must obey, not as obeying the prophet, but as obeying God Himself who has transmitted this message to them through the prophet." That distinction is important and necessary if we want to save our necks and possibly if we want to save our souls.

As long as the theory of Father Dhanis is able to be whispered in private rooms, as long as the theory that Fatima is only a "private revelation" which can be ig-nored with no consequences to yourself is not con-fronted and confounded, then, though the Church will survive until the end of time, there is a chance that a great portion of the Faithful will not survive with the Church.

The Faith in Crisis Around the World

In 1984, Bishop Cosme do Amaral, the Bishop of Fatima, said, "Apostasy of a nation is a greater disaster than the annihilation of a nation." He said that it was true that the Faith was diminishing more and more in Europe. Also in '84, Cardinal Ratzinger said, "The Faith is in crisis around the world." His book, which has gone into over a million copies in circulation in various languages, was published first in interview form in the magazine *Jesus* put out by the Pauline Sisters. Every word was published with his permission, then was made into a longer exposition in book form in June of the following year.

You can summarize that report in that one sentence, "The Faith is in crisis around the world." This is what the Holy Father was alluding to when he said, "Can the Mother Who, with all the force of love that She fosters in the Holy Spirit, Who desires everyone's salvation, remain silent...? No. She cannot remain silent."

But She is depending on Her bishop sons to not remain silent — to bring the full Message of Fatima to the faithful. That is why when Sister Lucy says, "The Blessed Virgin is very sad, because no one pays attention to Her message, not the bad nor the good." And that is why we see statues of Our Lady of Fatima and other statues of Our Lady weeping tears of water or tears of blood. There are many examples of them.

Pope John Paul II, speaking about Theresa Musco's statue said, "If the Blessed Virgin is crying, She must have a reason." Sister Lucy tells us the reason. Our Lady is very sad because no one pays attention to Her message, not the good, nor the bad. The bad, as Sister Lucy points out, are not seeing the chastisement of God fall upon them, and go on their merry way in sin. But She goes on to explain that not even the good are giving enough attention to Her full Fatima Message.

Simple Necessary Actions

I would not be doing you a service if I did not tell you the truth. I am only sorry that I am not better at explaining it. I really hope that you will not go away with some question that I have not covered. There are answers I can find for you. I have not yet found a question for which I have not been able to find an answer, a logical, theological answer which fits the facts and fits everything we know about the Message of Fatima. If the truth is not with me, then it will be a great service to me and to others to point it out to me. But if the truth is what I say, then we must act on it. Not simply in this room, not with a vote of thanks but with whatever power and authority God has given you in your diocese with your brother bishops, those who are here and those who are not here, as well as with the priests and faithful.

At least we could have a campaign of the Rosary, as Sister Lucy has said. Even by those so-called theologians who divide Fatima into One, Two, and Three, they acknowledge that the Rosary is a pious and holy thing to do. So at least if we cannot agree on anything else, we can have a campaign of the Rosary, around the world, for the good of the Church. We could have it also to save the Faithful from the dangers that Cardinal Ratzinger has warned about in his books and in his interviews about the crisis of the faith around the world.

Our Lady promised St. Dominic that the Rosary is a powerful weapon against Hell. It will overcome sin, decrease vice and overcome heresy. Those who pray the Rosary every day will not fall into heresy. If they should have the misfortune to fall into heresy, if they continue to pray the Rosary every day, they will get out of their heresy.

We are living in a time of great Apostasy. If it is not the Apostasy of Sacred Scripture it is a good dress rehearsal for it. In any case, this generation needs the Rosary, and needs to hear it from the bishops and priests also. But if the bishops will say so and continue to say so to more and more people, the others will finally continue to say this to the people more and more. The others will finally catch the idea and continue to repeat it.

Our Lady came to Fatima with a Scapular in Her hand. She held out the Scapular of Our Lady of Mount Carmel. As Sister Lucy has explained, Our Lady wants everyone to wear it. As Pope Pius XII said, "Let this be your personal sign of consecration to the Immaculate Heart of Mary." Sister Lucy has told us that the Scapular and the Rosary go together. I first put the Scapular on in Aylesford, in England, where Our Lady first appeared to St. Simon Stock in 1251. I was there for about six months. There I was enrolled in the Scapular in March of 1965, and since I put it on there have been very few days, perhaps less than 20 in the last 27 years, that I have not prayed at least five decades of the Rosary. This is one grace that accompanies the Scapular. By wearing the Scapular of Mount Carmel, which goes back to the time of the Prophet Elias, by entrusting ourselves to the Scapular protection, Our Lady accompanies this protection with the grace to pray the Rosary every day. That is why She came to Fatima with the Rosary in one hand and the Scapular in the other.

I have given away and enrolled in the Scapular hundreds of thousands of people but it is all too few for what must be done. Whatever I can do, you can do a hundred times more, simply because God has given you much more authority and a much stronger position from which to say what must be said.

Chapter 2

The Great Conspiracy

by Deirdre Manifold

Heaven's Queen. "Who is She that cometh forth as the morning, rising fair as the moon, bright as the sun, terrible as an army in battle array." Who is She? She is the woman of Genesis 3:15 about whom God spoke at the dawn of history, when He said, "I will put enmity between thee and the Woman, between your seed and Her seed. She will crush your head and you will lie in wait for Her heel."

What is that about, but war? War between Our Lady on one side and the serpent on the other side. Fatima is all about war, war for souls, and in the last analysis, it's each individual soul we are fighting for, in the name of Our Lady. This warfare began in Eden, as I've just said. Fatima is not just another apparition that we can take or leave. Fatima is for all mankind.

Fatima's Unquestionable Authenticity

We are the Church Militant and we have a duty to examine Fatima's authenticity. In order to show that the message came from Heaven, God was willing to perform an extraordinary miracle, the Miracle of the Sun. This was only the third time in history that God used the sun to make clear that the message was divine.

One was the prolongation of the daylight at the prayer of Joshua (Joshua 10) and the other was the sign given to the King of Judah in 714 B.C. by the prophet Isaias, when the sun retraced its path by ten hours. (4 Kings 20) What made the miracle of Fatima unique is that its time and place were prophesied months in advance.

The press, vehemently anti-clerical, sent its reporters to ridicule the predicted miracle which they expected to never take place. But they were the very people who wrote the most eloquent accounts of it. This miracle was witnessed by 70,000 people present at Fatima, and by many more on the perimeter (some as far as 25 miles away). And later was seen by Pius XII in the Vatican Gardens.

At Fatima, the Woman of Genesis had entered history in a most spectacular way. At Cana, when Mary noticed the wine had run short, Our Lord addressed Her as "Woman", saying "Woman, My hour has not yet come." But Mary was to precipitate His hour and in doing so Her hour had come. At that moment, She became the Woman of Genesis.

Her hour too had come and She would intervene in every crisis in the Church. For crisis there is today, probably as never before.

The Protestant Rebellion and its Consequences

The seeds of today's conflict were sown in the Reformation. Then it was rebellion against Peter, the Rock on which the Church is built. After the rebellion, what a change in every area of life! Up to then there were no standing armies and hardly a police force in the villages. If there were no police, the butcher was entitled to arrest anybody who had committed a crime. Just imagine life being so peaceful. The Monasteries looked after the poor, the sick, the widowed and the orphaned. No need for state institutions, and crippling taxes to ruin them. And just imagine, think about this — for four hundred years, the coin, the penny, in England and Ireland, retained the same value. From the year 1130 to 1530 there was no inflation. The same value all the time. Just imagine if we had that today; just think what

86

has happened the last few weeks, with money going up and down in value like a yo-yo. And of course, it's all a trick. It all comes from Satan.

Our Lord said "Seek ye first the Kingdom of God and all these things will be added." After that, man began to depend on himself. That great Englishman G.K. Chesterton used to say, "If we are not willing to be ruled by God then we will be ruled by tyrants."

On July 13, 1917, Our Lady showed the children a vision of Hell. "You have seen Hell where poor sinners go. In order to save them, God wishes to establish devotion to My Immaculate Heart." In mentioning that Russia would spread her errors throughout the world fomenting wars and revolution, She said She would come again to ask for the Consecration of Russia to Her Immaculate Heart by the Pope, in union with all the bishops of the world. Then Our Lady foretold World War II if people do not repent.

She said, "This event would be preceded by an unknown light." On January 25, 1938, this unknown light shone all across Europe for three hours. It could not be explained by the scientists, so strange a sight it was. It was reported in all the big daily newspapers of Europe at the time and even as far away as the *New York Times*.

Rakovsky

Now, immediately following the shining of this bright light, an event took place in Moscow which would directly trigger World War II. A man named Rakovsky, who had previously been Soviet Ambassador to both London and Paris, was being tried by Stalin in the purges of 1938. This man, Rakovsky, outlined a plan to Stalin's most trusted advisor, a man known as Gabriel, during a six-hour interview. The plan was that a friendship pact between Hitler and Stalin, then bitter enemies, be enacted, whereby they would join the attack and divide Poland between them. Following this, it could be arranged that the Allies would attack Hitler only (not Stalin) and later the United States would enter the war. To Gabriel, Stalin's confidant, this plan seemed ridiculous, impossible. He laughed at the idea of bringing Hitler and Stalin together for any purpose. But Rakovsky insisted and pointed out to Gabriel that Davis, the American Ambassador to Russia, was the person who would make the arrangements. Now, note this well, both Russia and America pushed Hitler into the war.

Rakovsky then revealed something that at the time was unknown to Gabriel and even to Stalin. He revealed that a higher order than that of Communism existed, whose orders would have to be obeyed. This bears out what Doctor Bella Dodd, head of the Communist Party in New York during the war had said. When she reported to Cleon Skousin, second in command of the FBI, she said that whenever she had any difficulty in getting instructions from Moscow because of the war, she was to go to any one of three wealthy capitalists in the Waldorf Towers. What amazed Doctor Dodd was that whenever these men gave instructions, Moscow always ratified them. When asked who the men were, Doctor Dodd refused to name them. But when pressed to say ultimately who ruled this higher order, she replied simply, "Satan."

In the course of this history-making interview, Rakovsky made it clear that the key to the power of this higher order was money. Rakovksy said, "Money is power, the only power."

Few people are aware also that three American presidents were assassinated because they dared to question the right of this private monopoly to make money with pen and ink out of nothing. Instead of borrowing as he was pressed to do, Abraham Lincoln issued greenbacks to pay the soldiers in the Civil War. No borrowing, no interest. McKinley spoke out against the monopoly and Kennedy actually issued United States dollars instead of Federal Reserve ones. Each President, Lincoln, McKinley, and Kennedy, in turn, were suddenly and ruthlessly murdered. And the press has never revealed this part of the plot. The media won't mention it. Because of the manipulation of money which is made into a commodity instead of the symbol that it is, the world everywhere is in turmoil.

Christ said that Satan was a liar from the beginning. Through this manipulation of money, Satan is also a thief. The Third World debt is crippling it, because the interest is so great. And the capital that was lent to them was made out of nothing but pen and ink. Because of this power to make money with pen and ink, governments everywhere can be ordered to legalize what is sinful — contraception, abortion, divorce.

I know from my own country that these demands do not come from the people. They are organized from outside and the people are told that they need them. Of course they will always get a vociferous minority very often of my own sex, women, feminists, who say that they must have them.

Now, who are these rulers? The English Prime Minister, Disraeli, in the last century was to say, "The world is ruled by very different people from what is imagined by those who are not behind the scenes." Our war is not with flesh and blood but with principalities and powers. The Church Militant has a duty to know and understand the enemy.

The Popes and Fatima

There are many apparitions world wide. Many are false. Human beings need great discernment when dealing with the practical jokes of a fallen angel. But there are many modern apparitions that do not require much discernment in order to figure out what they are all about. All you need is just common sense to know how ridiculous they are and compare them with Fatima. I am, of course, referring to the most famous false one taking place today. However, there could be no doubt whatever concerning the authenticity of the Fatima apparitions. They have been enthusiastically accepted by every Pope since Pius XI. And these Popes saw the Fatima apparitions as a warning to the people of the world to repent of their sins, as they were once warned at Nineveh when the King ordered everybody to pray and fast — even the very animals were fasting. The King himself got into sackcloth and ashes and prayed for nine days.

Pius XI responded with an Encyclical regarding Russia's errors, referred to by Our Lady. He said, "Communism is intrinsically evil, and no one who would save Christian civilization may collaborate with it in any undertaking whatsoever. For the evil we must combat is, at its origin, primarily, an evil of the spiritual order. From this polluted source, the monstrous emanations of the Communist system flow with satanic logic." So said Pius XI.

Next was Pope Pius XII who was to declare, "Fatima is the summation of my thinking. The time for doubting Fatima is passed. It is now time for action."

John XXIII instituted the Feast of Our Lady of the Rosary of Fatima and termed the Fatima apparitions, "the center of all Christian hope."

Paul VI, on November 21, 1964, solemnly renewed Pope Pius XII's consecration of the world to Mary's Immaculate Heart in the presence of all the Council Fathers. In 1967, on the occasion of the Golden Jubilee of the apparitions, he came here to Fatima in person as a humble pilgrim to pray for peace.

John Paul I as Cardinal Luciani expressed his recognition of the divine origin of the Fatima apparitions, and he sent a statue of Our Lady of Fatima around Italy later on.

On May 13, 1979, our present Holy Father, John Paul II sent a warm message emphasizing that conversion and penance were essential to the Fatima Message. On May 13, 1982, at Fatima, he thanked Our Lady for his survival despite the assassination bullets. He repeated the 1942 and 1964 consecrations of the world to Mary's Immaculate Heart, adding if the Church has accepted the Message of Fatima, it is above all, because the message contained a truth and a call whose basic content is the truth and the call of the Gospel itself.

Since it is pertinent that every Pope since Pius XI has accepted the Fatima Message as being genuine, why then is it that Fatima has not been preached from the housetops as it should have been? Had it been so preached from the housetops, grace would surely have flowed from Heaven to fulfill Our Lady's wishes. That it has not been so preached will not surprise anyone who sees the War in its true perspective, as War between the Woman of Genesis and the serpent, a creature of angelic intelligence.

The Deliberate Overthrow of Christ's Order

In war, above all else, we need to know the enemy. As members of the Church Militant we have a duty to study his plan and his tactics. Pope Leo XIII identified the enemy as Freemasonry, as will be explained later on.

In Matthew's opening chapter of the New Testament we read, verse 1, "The book of the generation of Jesus Christ, the son of David, the son of Abraham." Then, verse 20 refers to St. Joseph, "But while he thought on these things, behold the Angel of the Lord appeared to him in his sleep saying, 'Joseph, son of David, fear not to take unto thee Mary thy wife, for that which is conceived in Her is of the Holy Ghost'." Both these two spiritual sons of David are seen blessing the crowd at Fatima on the 13th of October. St. Joseph with the baby Jesus in his arms.

However, St. Paul sounds a warning when he says in Galatians 4 that, just as the spiritual Son was persecuted in olden times, so it is today. We further understand from St. Paul that this persecution is allegorical. Since only one of these spiritual sons of David is building the Temple of the Holy Ghost, we must establish the allegorical rival of this son and find in the Old Testament a type who, in addition to building the Temple, would also be the natural son of David. Such a man was Solomon. Allegorically speaking, who today is the capital enemy of Jesus Christ if not those building a temple in the name of Solomon? Associated with Solomon was the Knights Templar, who were sometimes called the Sons of Solomon. That Rosicrucian addict, Francis Bacon, in his book, *The New Atlantis,* conjured up a manifesto for the New Order, under the title of *Solomon's House.* The actual building of Solomon's Temple is the stated aim of that religion, which describes itself as "A system of morals veiled in allegory", and labelled by Pope Leo XIII as the capital enemy of the Church, commonly known as Freemasonry.

In his great encyclical *Humanum Genus*, Pope Leo XIII described it thus, "Tear away the mask of Freemasonry and make it plain to all what it is. It aims at the utter overthrow of the whole religious order of the world which Christian teaching has produced and the substitution of a new state of things based on the principles of pure naturalism. Including almost every nation in its grasp, it unites itself with other sects of which it is the real inspiration and the hidden motive of power. It first attracts and then retains its associates by the base of worldly advantage which it secures for them. It bends governments to its will, sometimes by promises, other times by threats. It has found its way into every class of society and forms an invisible and irresponsible power. An independent government, as it were, within the body of the lawful state. It denies that our first parents sinned and consequently that man's free will is in any way weakened or inclined to evil. We see that men are publicly tempted by many allurements of pleasure, there are journals or pamphlets without moderation or shame, stage plays are remarkably licentious. The designs of works of art are shamelessly sought in the laws of so-called realism. And all the blandishments of pleasure are diligently sought out by which virtue may be lulled to sleep. There have been in these secret societies some who are proposed artfully and of set purpose that the multitude should be satiated with boundless license of vice, as when this had been done it could come more easily under their power and authority." (*Humanum Genus* - Encyclical on Freemasonry)

The enemy could never win the battle by confronting the Church from the outside, he had to get right inside. Like a parasite eating at its host he had to eat it up from the inside. But we are promised that Our Lady will win. We can be joyful and hopeful because we know

She will crush his head. We don't know when it is going to take place, but it will happen. Our Lady has said, "My Immaculate Heart will triumph, in the end. The Consecration will be made, Russia will be converted and there will be peace."

However, I want to try to find out the nature of the enemy, what he is up to, how he acts, and the kind of organization he works through.

Our Lady will Crush the Serpent

There is an organization in our society that claims to have the treasure of Solomon's Temple. Now the supreme order marshalling all these forces striving to build the Temple of Solomon is known as the *Ordo Templi Orientis*. Its goal is to establish the Phallic religion in place of Christianity. Foremost among its many sub-groups is a body calling itself the Gnostic Catholic Church. The Creed of the Gnostic Catholic Church contains the words, "I believe in the serpent and the lion."

That a body calling itself the Gnostic Catholic Church should be the chief antagonist against the Mystical Body of Christ ought not to surprise us, for this is the organic type of war whereby the seed of the serpent will seek to destroy the Mystical Body of Christ from within as a parasite would destroy its host body, the body that sustains it.

Here now we see the martial decree of Genesis 3:15: "I will put enmity between thee and the Woman ..." It is depicted on the Tilma of Juan Diego in Guadalupe and later on the front of the Miraculous Medal, war between the seed of the Woman and the serpent. Our Lady stands on the serpent in both the Tilma and in the Miraculous Medal, the front of the Miraculous Medal. On the back, as you know, there are two Hearts, Our Lord's and Our

Lady's, with the sword through it, confirming what Simon said, "Thine own soul a sword shall pierce."

Now as to the immediate outcome of this warfare we can call to mind the words of St. Louis de Montfort. He said, "Things will become progressively worse until the coming of the Antichrist." Now all efforts to fight the enemy would seem to be futile unless the proper consecration of Russia, as ordered by Our Lady, to the Immaculate Heart of Mary be made in the near future. To make this consecration exactly as Our Lady requested, after the lapse of sixty-three years, would prove that we are, after all, teachable.

As you know, on June 13, 1929, Lucy had a marvellous apparition of the Blessed Trinity and Our Lady. Our Lady said the time had now come to ask for the consecration of Russia to Her Immaculate Heart. Now that was sixty-three years ago. The teaching office of the Church is related to all the nations of the world.

Foot Soldiers of Mary

In the land of modern Galatians, Ireland, in a church dedicated as a house of prayer to all the nations of the world, on August 21, 1879, on the gable end of this church, appeared St. Joseph, that other spiritual son of David. He was contemplating the allegorical warfare directed against the high priesthood of Jesus Christ. The apparition showed a live lamb on an altar from which rose a cross, the whole surrounded by adoring angels.

To the left was St. John with a missal in his hand, two fingers raised, warning of that which looks like a lamb and speaks like a dragon. Between St. Joseph and St. John stood Mary. The whole vision was above the ground.

I refer, of course, to the apparition of the Lamb of God at Knock, Ireland. Now it would appear that St. Joseph was looking at this allegorical warfare, at Our Lady in the center, at St. John, warning that there was a lamb that looked like a lamb but spoke like a dragon right within the Church. This was a visible apparition, (seen by many) in my country of Ireland. But later on there was an invisible apparition of Our Lady. On the evening of September 7, 1921, the eve of Her birthday, Mary came again to Ireland. This time, as I said, it was in an invisible manner, but no less real. When guiding a small group of women and one man who came to pray for sinners, She instituted Her spiritual army, since known as the Legion of Mary.

The Legion of Mary seeks through Mary to bring Christ to every nation, through the personal sanctification of each member of the Legion. This spiritual army seeks to gain the whole world for Mary and was mainly responsible for the preservation of the Church in China. Though the Legion of Mary was established only in 1921, already three of its members have their cause for canonization going ahead: Edele Quinn, who was an envoy to Africa for seven years, in the 30's and 40's; Alfie Lamb, a young man of only 25, who went to South America where he lived only about six years before he died of cancer; and Frank Duff, who died in 1980.

This is the spiritual army that is fighting the serpent on the ground.

We are all foot soldiers of Mary. There's no time for being neutral. You are either with Christ or against Him. Now I would say regarding the place where I'm standing, two small nations, Portugal and Ireland, have been chosen by God at this moment of peril to lead mankind back to sanity.

The Social Teaching of the Church

The answer to Russia's errors are clearly set out in the Encyclicals *Rerum Novarum, Quadragesimo Anno, Divini Redemptoris,* and in many other social encyclicals. The answer to Russia's errors are also found in the writings of Father Denis Fahey, a Holy Ghost priest from Ireland who has written about the Kingship of Christ, the Mystical Body of Christ and its place in the world to ordinary lay people who are often uninstructed in these matters.

The encyclicals and these writings of Father Fahey are the antidote to the poison of the Karl Marx manifesto.

Some years ago I was exasperated by meeting so many university students who talked about Karl Marx as if he were a saint, greater than Christ. They thought Marx was a great intellectual who yearned for the freedom of men, to make people free. I asked some friends who supply me with books from America to please send me a handy life of Karl Marx. I never received it. I wanted to give the book to those university students. Then I happened to be in America and asked some friends "When are you going to produce this life of Karl Marx that I can give to the students to let them know what kind a man he really was?" One of them turned to me and said, "Why don't you write it yourself?" Well I felt inadequate. I knew Marx was a bad man because of what Communism had done in the world, but I really knew very little about him. I gathered incentive for this project by going back to my training in the Legion of Mary. Frank Duff taught us that if we were called to do something, we should step forward in faith, walk on the water, go as far as possible, and then God would step in.

So I went home and I said, "well, what would I do if I wanted to write the life of Karl Marx?" I knew nothing about him. So I inaugurated my research. In about a year and a half I had finished writing my book *Karl Marx, True or False Prophet?* It was difficult work, much harder than my first book, *Fatima and The Great Conspiracy*, but at least it gives people an idea of what kind of man he was, a satanist, an enemy of the Church.

I am convinced that students in school ought to be as familiar with the Social Teaching of the Church as they are familiar with the Our Father. The problem, however, is that students do not know anything about the Social Teaching of the Church. I didn't know it existed. I didn't know anything about Father Fahey and his wonderful writings on the Mystical Body of Christ and on the Kingship of Christ. Things are so bad in the schools nowadays that children are making their First Communion and going to confession without knowing the Ten Commandments. These things need to be pointed out. Over the last couple of days since I arrived, ideas have been tumbling into my mind that would take too long to state here. I hope I may one day return and talk to you about them, maybe off the cuff this time. What I would say to you now is that the children ask for bread and they are given stones. Today the sheep are hungry, the lambs are starving. My lords, the future is up to you.

Chapter 3

The Plot to Silence Our Lady

by Father Paul Leonard Kramer

The question of the Consecration of Russia requested by Our Lady of Fatima is a very simple question, simple enough that a person can be mystified when he encounters the controversy there has been over the last seven years about whether it has or has not been done. I do not believe a controversy could exist if all would examine the matter very carefully.

It reminds me of when I was still a boy in school and one of my teachers spoke about the great controversy over the number of teeth in a horse's mouth, how there were great debates and learned discourses determining what must be the number of teeth in the horse's mouth. Finally someone decided well, let's open the horse's mouth and count.

The question of the Consecration of Russia is as simple as opening up the horse's mouth and counting its teeth, unless, of course, there are some ulterior motives for creating a controversy over this question.

Few who have heard the Message of Our Lady of Fatima have been able to fully grasp the gravity of the warning that the Blessed Virgin addressed to the world. All too often people consider it to be simply a call to conversion or a mere private revelation with which they need not concern themselves. They accept that Our Lady of Fatima came in 1917 on six successive months, and She eventually promised peace to the world, and they leave it at that. They forget what is at the heart of the Message of Fatima. The heart of the Fatima Message is contained in the Secret, that God is going to punish the world by means of war, hunger, persecution of the Church and of the Holy Father. To prevent it Our Lady says, "I shall come to ask for the Consecration of Russia to My Immaculate Heart and the Communion of Reparation on the First Saturdays. If they attend to My requests, Russia will be converted and the world will have peace. If not, Russia will spread its errors throughout the world, raising up wars and persecutions of the Church. The good will be martyred, the Holy Father will have much to suffer, and various nations will be annihilated. In the end, My Immaculate Heart will triumph, the Holy Father will consecrate Russia to Me, it will be converted and a period of peace will be granted to the world."

This is, of course, a well known text of that part of the Secret that has been officially revealed. In this segment Our Blessed Mother is saying that the human race has two options. We can obey Her requests, in which case, these evils will be prevented. She says, "To prevent it, I shall come to ask for the Consecration of Russia to My Immaculate Heart." Therefore, She makes it very clear that if the Consecration of Russia is carried out these evils will not take place. And so the option we have is further wars, hunger, persecution of the Church and the Holy Father and the errors of Russia spread throughout the world, then the triumph of the Immaculate Heart of Mary, or else, we can have the Consecration done first. We can avoid war, hunger, persecution of the Church and the Holy Father.

There are some who claim that the Consecration of Russia has already been properly performed. If this claim were correct, then the possibility of nuclear, chemical or biological war would no longer exist for our generation. If their claim is correct then there cannot be any more famine in our century. If what they claim is true then it is no longer possible for our genera-

tion to be dominated by the powerful and mighty pluto-
crats, the financiers of the international banks who
oppress entire nations, reduce rich nations to poverty
and reduce poor nations to grinding poverty. If the Consecration is done then these things cannot be happening.

A Grand Folly

Last February there was a full page advertisement in
the *Manila Bulletin* taken from a Blue Army publication in Spain. It announced that the Consecration of
Russia has been done and therefore there was no longer
the possibility of a world war. A greater folly than this is
hard to conceive. God has unconditionally promised
that the horrors that Our Lady mentioned will not take
place. Our Blessed Mother Herself said that these
things will be prevented by the Consecration of Russia,
but we can see today the world is headed toward the
abyss. From one day to the next the situation in the
world becomes worse. And yet there are some, like Father Miller of the Blue Army, like Bishop Luna of the
Blue Army, and Father Fox, formerly of the Blue Army,
who are saying that the Consecration is already done
and that what we see in our day is the beginning of the
triumph of the Immaculate Heart of Mary. We see such
an abundance of sin in the world, every kind of vice, every kind of corruption in private and public life, injustice abounds and entire nations and classes of people are
being oppressed. If this is the beginning of the Triumph
of the Immaculate Heart of Mary, then I shudder to
think of what that triumph would be at the height of its
glory.

What we see happening today cannot possibly be the
Triumph of the Immaculate Heart of Mary. The thought
borders on blasphemy, because what we see today is the
domination of evil in the world. Such a triumph would

be a triumph of evil over good. But Our Lady came to Fatima precisely with the message of hope, that indeed it will be the contrary.

"In the end, My Immaculate Heart will triumph, the Pope will consecrate Russia to Me and a period of peace will be given to the world."

We do not have peace in the world today. Peace is, as defined by St. Augustine, the tranquility of order, and there can only be peace in the world when the social order is restored according to the eternal law of God.

An Evil Empire

The sect of Freemasonry has been active for many centuries.

They surfaced and became public in the year 1717. Since then they have made ceaseless war and revolution. To use the words of the Communists, they have made total war — political, intellectual, economic, every sort of war imaginable — in order to completely invert the social order, to destroy the authority of Jesus Christ and His Church, to take God off of His throne, and to deify man. We see the progress, the motion toward accomplishing this evil empire, the empire of the Antichrist. Every day it seems to be coming closer and closer. This cannot possibly be confused with the triumph promised by Our Lady, which will be the Triumph of Faith, the triumph of the one true religion. Therefore, I think, for that consideration alone, one must, at least if not having examined the facts about the Consecration of Russia, at this point in time, suspect that it has not yet been accomplished.

In 1917, Our Lady said She would simply come again and She would ask for the Consecration of Russia. The Secret was not for 1917. Our Lady did not explain in any great detail what She would ask for. That came later. On June 13, 1929, Our Lady appeared to Sister Lucy. She said that God is now asking for the Consecration of Russia and here She specified precisely what it is that God wants.

There are two versions given by Sister Lucy of the words that Our Lady spoke to her on that occasion. One clarifies the other. The first text reads, "The moment has come in which God asks the Holy Father, in union with all the bishops of the world, to consecrate Russia to My Immaculate Heart, promising to save it by this means." Another text also straight from the hand of Sister Lucy reads, "The moment has come in which God asks the Holy Father to make and to order that, in union with him, and at the same time, all the bishops of the world make the consecration of Russia to My Immaculate Heart." Our Lady added that, "by this means Russia will be saved."

Consecration is an Honor, Not an Insult

Before going any further, I want to say that this would be a great act of charity to Russia. Russia is undergoing a tribulation in these days, great disorder, hunger, upheaval. In the past, some of the advisors of the Holy Father suggested to him that he not consecrate Russia by name because they thought that this would be perceived by the Soviets as an insult, a provocation. The same objection was made to Pope Pius XII. He did not think it would be any provocation at all. He simply disregarded the advice and he went on by himself to make a consecration of Russia and, of course, there were no terrible consequences. The Soviets did not understand that to be any kind of insult. There were no repercussions against the Church. Yet this argument has been used time and again to tie the Holy Father's hands so that he will not consecrate Russia.

Even very recently it has been stated again by certain officials of the Secretariat of State that this consecration of Russia is no longer needed. They still believe that it will be perceived as an insult to Russia. Whereas entirely the contrary is the case. If you pray for someone you are doing them an act of kindness. You are honoring them and if setting them aside with a solemn prayer of consecration, you are honoring them in a special way. When David was set aside from his brothers and anointed, this was certainly no insult to David.

Yet it is still perceived by some that this solemn Act of Consecration would somehow be considered an insult to the Russian people. I do not see how a healthy mind can conceive of it in this manner.

Due to these political considerations, there has been a great deal of propaganda to try and completely confuse and obscure the issue about the Consecration of Russia to the Immaculate Heart of Mary.

Father Gruner has already mentioned that the Vatican-Moscow Agreement has been and remains the great stumbling block. There have been some practical repercussions as a result of this agreement. We can recall that when Cardinal Ratzinger issued a warning about the Theology of Liberation, Cardinal Casaroli, at that time the Secretariat of State, publicly distanced himself from the declaration. The Holy Father himself spoke about the evils of communism although not using those words. So did Cardinal Ratzinger. Cardinal Ratzinger has himself admitted that the consecration of Russia has not yet been done. The Holy Father has publicly acknowledged that Our Blessed Lady is still waiting for the consecration. But even in Rome there has been some division on this matter.

When asked, Cardinal Casaroli does not speak about the consecration of Russia. Nevertheless, there is a great deal of pressure being exerted to get people to say that it has been done in spite of the fact that:

1) the Holy Father has stated that Our Lady is still waiting for the consecration, and
2) Cardinal Ratzinger has bluntly stated that it is not yet done.

This is the source of the controversy about the consecration. The matter is as clear as the light of day, simple as counting the teeth in the horse's mouth. That is what we are going to do right now.

The Facts Concerning the Consecration of Russia

More than once in my articles in *The Fatima Crusader* I have presented facts to demonstrate beyond any shadow of a doubt that Our Lady's request for the consecration of Russia has not yet been done. Those publications and organizations that wish to uphold the Vatican-Moscow Agreement have not responded except to answer with deception.

The first fact I have already presented, the words of the Queen of Heaven Herself, when She said that "the moment has come in which God asks the Holy Father to make and to order that, in union with him, and at the same time, all the bishops of the world make the consecration of Russia to My Immaculate Heart." It is well known that this event has not taken place, namely all the bishops in the world have not performed, together with the Pope, a ceremony consecrating Russia to the Immaculate Heart of Mary. I should add that it was mentioned in many newspapers throughout the world on March 25, 1984, that the Pope did consecrate the world. No television networks, no wire services, no newspaper reported any consecration of Russia.

It is the common and correct perception that what

took place was the consecration of the world because the Holy Father made no mention of Russia, neither on March 25, 1984, nor in his earlier consecration of the world made at Fatima in 1982. In neither of these acts of consecration did he make any mention of Russia.

The second fact to be considered is the text that Sister Lucy wrote to Father Gonçalves in 1930. She wrote, "The good God promises to make an end of the persecution of Russia if the Holy Father deigns to make and orders to be made by all the bishops of the Catholic world, the solemn and public act of reparation and consecration of Russia." In a letter of June 12, 1930, she said, "If only the Holy Father will himself make a solemn act of reparation and consecration of Russia as well as ordering all the bishops of the Catholic world to do the same."

On March 21, 1982, Sister Lucy declared in the presence of the Apostolic Nuncio to Lisbon, Archbishop Portalupi, in the presence of the Bishop of Leiria and Dr. Lacerda, that the Pope must select a date on which to order the bishops of the world to make a public and solemn act of reparation and consecration of Russia.

On the afternoon of March 19, 1983, the Apostolic Nuncio, Archbishop Portalupi, met with Sister Lucy in order to establish precisely what Sister Lucy had to say concerning the consecration of the world that the Pope had performed on May 13, 1982. There were other witnesses present. Sister Lucy declared that the consecration of Russia had not been made as Our Lady had demanded and she added, "I could not say so because I did not have the permission of the Holy See."

So, you see, she could not speak openly on this matter at that time because she needed the permission of the Holy See. She was under obedience to be silent about this question. The Pope's consecration of the world on March 25, 1984, did not clearly indicate Russia as its object and the bishops did not participate in a public and solemn ceremony.

The reasons Sister Lucy gave in 1982 specify likewise why the consecration of 1984 was deficient. On July 20, 1987, Sister Lucy stated to Enrico Romero, in a subsequently published interview that the consecration of Russia requested by Our Lady of Fatima is not yet done.

In an interview which appeared in the September 1985 issue of *Sol de Fatima,* Sister Lucy was asked if the Pope had fulfilled the request made by Our Lady at Tuy when he consecrated the world in 1984. Sister Lucy answered, "There has been no participation of all the bishops, and there was no mention of Russia." The interviewer then asked, "So the consecration was not done as requested by Our Lady?" Sister Lucy answered, "No, many bishops attached no importance to this act."

Finally John Paul II, on March 25, 1984, after he had consecrated the world, twice addressed words to Our Lady of Fatima, words which contained a clear admission that the consecration She requested still remained to be done. His words were published in *L 'Osservatore Romano,* and he said, "Enlighten especially the peoples of which You, Yourself, are awaiting our consecration and confiding."

Several hours later the Holy Father again addressed Our Lady of Fatima in St. Peter's Basilica with these words, "We wish to choose this Sunday for the Act of Entrusting and Consecration of the world, of all peoples, especially those who have a very great need of this consecration and entrusting, of those people for whom You, Yourself, are awaiting our act of consecration."

These public statements of the Holy Father clearly

demonstrate that he himself is aware of the fact that Our Lady of Fatima is still waiting for the consecration of Russia to be performed.

If Russia is consecrated as Our Lady requested, those evils — war, hunger, persecution of the Church and persecution of the Holy Father — will be prevented. She also stated that if it is not done, then Russia will spread its errors throughout the entire world and Russia would raise up wars and persecution.

The Red Mask

Many people have become complacent since the alleged dissolution of the Soviet Union. They think that since Russia is no longer officially and formally Marxist, therefore Russia is no longer a problem for world peace. One must consider the fact that the Soviet Union was not founded by true believers in the pure doctrine of Karl Marx. The doctrine of Marx was a mask. It was a mask to hide the true purpose of the Soviet Revolution.

The October Revolution was a masonic revolution. Lenin and Trotsky were both Freemasons of the 33rd degree. Communism was not created by political theorists but by masonic sectaries, whose purpose was to exterminate the Christian religion by first overthrowing the Christian monarchies, abolishing international boundaries, and erecting a Godless one-world republic.

Communism is not a mere social revolution. It is a masonic revolution whose purpose is to carry out Freemasonry's stated program to abolish all governments, property, and religion, and to build a new Godless order on the ruins of the old order.

Richard Wurmbrandt, who has studied carefully the writings of Karl Marx and who, himself, had been tortured terribly in the prison camps of the communists, wrote in his book, *Was Karl Marx a Satanist?* — "The ultimate aim of communism is not to establish another social or economic system, it is to mock God and praise Satan."

Now that Russia is no longer officially communist, one must not forget that Russia is still in the grips of masonic leaders. They may have changed the description of what they are doing, they may have changed the shell, but the substance remains.

In *The Fatima Crusader,* Josyp Terelya says that Russia is still deeply in the grips of Freemasonry. Nothing essential has really changed. The program of Masonry has been carried out openly for the last 200 years. The Patriarchs of Freemasonry commissioned Adam Weishaupt to establish a masonic sect called the Order of the Illuminati on May 1, 1776. The sect operated according to their program to abolish religion, property, and government. The Order and its devilish plans were discovered by the Bavarian government in 1785 and the Illuminati was scattered and regrouped under the name, The League of Just Men. Weishaupt died in 1830 but the Order survived. Later they changed their name to the League of Communists and they commissioned a document called the Communist Manifesto. Eventually they called themselves the Communist Party. Karl Marx became their official theoretician, and it is in the writings of Marx that we find exposed the true purpose of communism.

It is very interesting when you consider that the program and purpose of communism is identical to the program of Freemasonry and is also identical to the program of International Zionism. The deeper you examine these organizations the more you see that they have the self-same program and the self-same purpose. And they are all demonic.

The Devil's Poet

In a poem entitled *Invocation of One in Despair,* Karl Marx wrote, "I wish to avenge myself against the one who rules above. A God has snatched from me my all, in the curse and rock of destiny. Nothing but revenge is left to me." In another poem called, *The Prayer*, Marx says, "The vapors of hell rise and fill my brain until I go mad and my Heart is utterly changed. See this sword, the prince of darkness sold it to me."

In another poem called *The Invocation*, Marx makes the words of Lucifer his own, just like we read in Isaiah; "I will ascend into Heaven, I will exalt my throne above the stars of God". In *The Invocation,* Marx says, "I shall build my throne high overhead, cold, tremendous shall its summit be, for its bulwark, superstitious dread, for its marshall, blackest agony."

We can already see his program through these poetic terms. Superstitious dread, of course, is the satanic cult of the secret societies and by blackest agony, he means the cruel tyranny that will destroy all religious, civil and human rights. It will be total tyranny. Of course God answered to Lucifer in the above cited verse of Isaiah, "How thou art fallen from Heaven, O Lucifer, thou shalt be brought down to hell in the depth of the pit."

Similarly Karl Marx recognized that his destiny was the same. In a poem with a very strange name *Oulanem*, Marx writes, "Ruined, ruined, my time has clean run out. Soon I shall embrace eternity to my breast and soon I shall howl gigantic curses on mankind." In the same poem Marx writes, "Ah, eternity, she is our eternal grief". And, "indescribable and immeasurable death, ourselves being clockwork, blindly mechanical, having no purpose save to happen, to be ruined, so there shall be something to ruin."

Marx, like other satanists, loved to use inversion,

and thus is the strange name Oulanem. It is the inversion of the prophetic name given by Isaiah to Jesus Christ — Emanuel. You spell it backwards, then you reverse the syllables, and then you spell that backwards, and you have changed Emanuel into Oulanem. It is a triple reversal of Emanuel.

In another poem called, *The Pale Maiden,* Marx says, "Thus Heaven I forfeited, I know it full well, my soul once faithful to God, is chosen for Hell."

In these poems Marx states the true purpose of his life's work. "Soon I shall howl gigantic curses on mankind. If there is something which devours, I'll leap within in. Though I bring the world to ruins, the world which bulks between me and the abyss, I will smash to pieces with enduring curses. I'll throw my arms around its harsh reality. Embracing me the world will dumbly pass away and then sink down to utter nothingness. Perished."

These are the words of Karl Marx and you can find them with all the references to the original text of Marx in Richard Wurmbrandt's book, *Was Karl Marx a Satanist?*

It is essential, Richard Wurmbrandt points out, to state emphatically that Marx and his confreres, while anti-God, were not atheists as they publicly pretended to be. They hated a God in whom they believed. Marx's philosophy is a deliberate inversion of the truth. Marx was fascinated with the inversion that is common to satanists. Inversions so permeated Marx's whole manner of thinking, says Wurmbrandt, that he used them everywhere. He answers Proudhon's book *The Philosophy of Misery* with another book entitled *The Misery of Philosophy.* He also wrote, "We have to use instead of the weapon of criticism, the criticism of weapons." In other words, very clearly on other occasions, Marx said that their purpose was not to explain history but to change it. Therefore, truth is settled by arms, if someone disagrees with you, you shoot them and they're gone. This is, "the criticism of weapons."

Consequently, while Marx's doctrine teaches that, "man is a supreme being for man," and this is a direct quotation from his work, *Zur Kritik der Hegelschen Rechtsphilosophie*, he says that the suppression of religion as an illusory happiness of the people is a pre-supposition of true happiness. So, on the one hand, Karl Marx is saying that in order to liberate the human race we must get rid of the illusory happiness promised by religion. But in reality, in his poems Marx states his true purpose which is the eternal ruin and the destruction of the human race and the entire world.

According to Marx's doctrine of communism, the ultimate purpose of the socialist revolution is to emancipate man by suppressing religion. As he stated, "the critique of Heaven transforms itself into the critique of earth, the critique of theology into the critique of politics. Thus the fight against religion is indirectly the fight against the world of which religion is the spiritual aroma."

This means that since God is an illusion for Marx, man must be the supreme being for man. Christian civilization must be overthrown and destroyed in order to abolish and exterminate religion from the face of the earth. Thus we see that the communist program is identical to the program of Freemasonry, whose stated program is to destroy governments and altars.

The Communist movement is really a camouflaged version of the Masonic revolution. It presents itself to the world as the class struggle of the proletariat but underneath the shell there is nothing but the identical program of Freemasonry to abolish religion, to mock God, and to adore satan.

Heaven's Response

Lenin established Russia as the headquarters of the world revolution against religion. But God elected the Russian nation for a holy purpose. This is why Our Lady of Fatima revealed that the Pope and the bishops must consecrate Russia to the Immaculate Heart of Mary. This consecration is the only way that Russia will be solemnly established in its God-given vocation; a vocation which is entirely opposite to what Lenin had planned.

Russia is in a terrible condition and things will certainly become worse. But Our Blessed Mother says that God promises to save Russia by means of the Collegial Consecration requested at Fatima. As Our Lady Herself said, "He promises to save Russia by this means." In Fatima the Mother of God revealed what must be done in order to obtain the conversion of Russia and world peace. She has spoken elsewhere about the same problem of Russia. As Cardinal Ratzinger stated, "The Secret of Fatima corresponds to what has been revealed in many other Marian apparitions." Josyp Terelya himself has seen the Blessed Virgin when She appeared in Hrushiv, Ukraine. Here is part of what She said to him. "How many warnings will mankind be given before it repents? But the world continues in its self-will and hedonism. Oppression and war are the never-ending preoccupation of people. Russia continues to refuse to recognize My Son. She rejects true charity and continues to live its demonic existence. Did I not ask for prayers for the lost Russian people on other occasions?" Here I can add, "Yes." She asked precisely that at Fatima. She continued, "If Russia does not accept Christ the King, the entire world faces ruin. Antichrist has power and is opposed to the will of the Eternal One. The Antichrist is sowing envy and dissension."

We can recall how Sister Lucy on various occasions was questioned about the Secret. Since she could not reveal precisely its contents, she simply said, "It is in Sacred Scripture. It is in the Apocalypse." And she singled out chapters 8 to 13. What we read in those chapters is the establishment of the worldwide evil empire of the Antichrist; political, economic, military, and religious tyranny to establish the kingdom of Satan in the world, to remove God as the object of the worship of the human race and to put Satan in the place of God through his visible representative, the Antichrist.

Cardinal Ratzinger has stated that the revelation of Fatima corresponds to many previous apparitions of Our Lady. In fact, it corresponds to what has been foretold for many centuries by the Saints.

St. Methodius who died in 385 A.D. said, "A time will come when enemies of Christ will boast, we have subjected the earth and all its inhabitants and the Christians cannot escape our hands." The Venerable Bartholomeus Holzhauser, who died in 1658, wrote in his commentary on the Apocalypse, "When everything has been ruined by war, when Catholics are hard pressed by traitorist co-religionists and heretics, when the Church and her servants are denied their rights, the monarchies have been abolished and their rulers murdered, then the hand of the Almighty will work a marvellous change." Something apparently impossible according to human understanding.

Significant is the prophecy of Bishop George Michael Wittman who died in 1833. He said, "Woe is me, sad days are at hand for the Holy Church of Jesus Christ. The Passion of Jesus Christ will be renewed in the most dolorous manner in the Church and in her supreme head. In all parts of the world there will be wars and revolutions and much blood will be shed. Distress, disasters and poverty will be everywhere great since pestilential maladies, scarcity, and other misfortunes will follow one after another. Violent hands will be laid on the supreme head of the Catholic Church, bishops and priests will be persecuted and schism will be provoked and confusion reign amid all classes. Times will become so preeminently bad that it will seem as if the enemies of Christ and His Holy Church which He founded with His Blood were about to overcome Her. Secret societies will wreak great ruin and exercise a marvellous military power, and through that many will be blinded and infected with the most horrible errors. However, all this shall avail nought. They cannot shake the rock whereon Christ has founded His Church."

Blessed Anna Maria Taigi who died in 1837 prophesied and said, "God will ordain two punishments. One in the form of wars, revolution and other evils. The other will be sent from Heaven. There shall come over all the earth an intense darkness lasting three days and three nights. Nothing will be visible and the air will be laden with pestilence which will claim principally but not exclusively the enemies of religion."

Something of this nature we also see is foretold in the Old Testament. "The sun will lose its light." And this also seems to be corresponding to a very apocalyptic book, the Book of the Prophet Joel. The warning that Our Lady made at Fatima indicates, unlike prophecies of the saints who foretold these things to take place in a later age, that these things are now about to take place and She provided us with a remedy; the only remedy that will work to prevent these things happening in our generation.

In 1945, only a few months after World War II had

ended, when many people thought that the tribulation for some time at least would be over, Pope Pius XII stated in his Christmas message to the Cardinals, "The world is on the verge of a frightful abyss. Men must prepare themselves for suffering such as mankind has never seen."

On November 11, 1984, Cardinal Ratzinger stated in his interview that the things contained in the Third Secret correspond to what has been announced in Scripture and what has been said again and again in many Marian apparitions. I would like to quote one of those apparitions which has been formally approved by the Church.

In the city of Quito, Ecuador, a church was built in honor of this apparition. It is called "Our Lady of Good Fortune". On February 2, 1634, the Mother of God revealed to Mother Marianna de Jesus Torres, "At the end of the 19th Century and for a large part of the 20th, various heresies will flourish on this earth. The precious light of the Faith will go out in souls because of the almost total moral corruption. In those times, there will be great physical and moral calamities in private and in public. The little number of souls keeping the Faith and practicing the virtues will undergo cruel and unspeakable suffering. Through their drawn out martyrdom, many of them will go to their death because of the violence of their sufferings and those will count as martyrs who give their lives for Church or for country. To escape from being enslaved by these heresies will call for great strength of will, constancy, courage and great trust in God, all of which are gifts from the merciful Love of My Divine Son to those He will have chosen for the work of restoration. There will come moments when everything seems lost and paralyzed, and just then comes the beginning of the complete restoration.

Having gained control of all social classes, the sects will tend to penetrate with great skill into the heart of families and destroy even the children. The innocence of childhood will almost disappear, thus priestly vocations will be lost. It will be a real disaster. Priests will abandon their duties and will depart from the path marked out for them by God. Then the Church will go through a dark night for lack of a Prelate Father to watch over it with love, gentleness, strength, and prudence, and numbers of priests will lose the spirit of God, thus placing their souls in great danger. To scatter these black clouds blocking the brilliant dawning of the freedom of the Church there will be a terrible war in which the blood of priests and religious will flow. That night will be so horrible that wickedness will seem triumphant. Then will come My time. In astounding fashion I shall destroy satan's pride, casting him beneath My feet, chaining him up in the depths of hell, leaving Church and country freed at last from his cruel tyranny."

St. Hildegard of Bingham who died in 1189 wrote, "People will renounce the authority of the Pope. Individual countries will prefer their own church rulers to the Pope."

As Venerable Holzhauser said, "Catholics will be hard pressed by traitorists, co-religionists and heretics." Here we see foretold division in the Church. St. Hildegard said these things would take place and gave the sign to watch for when these things will take place. She said - after Germany will have been divided, and, of course, Germany was divided after the Second World War.

We have seen a profound crisis engulf and paralyze the Church from within. Father Cornelio Fabro, one of the most respected scholars of the Catholic world, pointed out in his work, "The Church is presently undergoing the gravest crisis that it has ever faced in its history."

Pope Paul VI himself lamented the fact that the Church seemed to be undergoing its own auto-demolition.

Masonry wishes to destroy the Catholic religion in order to establish a New World Order with a devilish religion throughout the world. This will be the basis for the worldwide rule of the Antichrist. Our Lady of Fatima says that She alone can help us. Those were Her words.

Political and military means will not be enough. As Our Lord said, "Those who use the sword will die by the sword." It is written in Sacred Scripture in the book of the Apocalypse, "It will be by the Faith and the patience of the saints that the wicked empire of the Antichrist will be overcome and by obedience to God's will." At Fatima Our Lady indicated that this will materialize in the Consecration of Russia to Her Immaculate Heart. She alone can help us.

Chapter 4

Prophetic Principle
and Priestly Tradition

by Fr. Paul Trinchard

Prophecy is God's corrective word to man. We have the prophetic principle and the priestly tradition. Priestly tradition is supposed to keep what God gives. In fact, to pass it on. The prophetic principle corrects and applies and makes well the present situation. Is the Fatima Message an absolutely-to-be-obeyed prophetic message and command from God, or is it something optional? That is the question that has to always be in our minds.

Three Criteria for True Prophecy

The criteria for a prophetic message first of all is that it has to claim to be from God for us. As God said in the Old Testament, false prophets spoke in their own name, they didn't speak in the name of God. He said to reject them. Second, the prophecy has to be proved. It is like a science, you have to prove that you speak from God. In the Old Testament, if a "prophet" makes a short-term prediction and it doesn't come true, he is to be taken out and stoned to death. The third criteria is that it has to agree with all of God's revelation. It has to agree with the Holy Bible and all that the Catholic Church teaches in its core and essential teachings.

Catholic post-biblical prophecy must and does highlight the Bible because Church doctrine comes from the Holy Bible. It follows that Biblical standards for judging the genuineness of prophecy must be applied to all modern apparitions. At Fatima, in 1917, 70,000 people saw the miracle, as predicted, on October 13. By contrast, in regard to Medjugorje, Bishop Zanic said, "We have been waiting for years. No sign, no proof." Bishop Zanic's criteria for Medjugorje is quite biblical. He knows that you must have proof. It must be a public proof. That is one of the criteria for authentic prophecy, and Fatima has it galore. Our Blessed Virgin Mary predicted a war under a Pope who was not there at the time, Pope Pius XI. She predicted a light shining in the sky in Europe. When it happened, on January 25, 1938, this light lasted three hours.

Consecration and Reparation

The last sermon I gave in church, the pastor was away. When he returned, he demanded my faculties be removed because I preached the pure Fatima Message. The fundamental message still remains the same, the consecration and reparation. These have a private dimension. Ultimately the consecration is for us individuals. Reparation also is for individuals primarily and ultimately. Yet it also has an ecclesial dimension. Father Gruner emphasizes the ecclesial and prophetic dimension. My focus, however, is mostly on reparation.

All the pieces will be in place when the Third Revelation of Fatima is disclosed. It's the Third Revelation, I refuse to call it a secret because the Blessed Virgin Mary does not play games. She doesn't say "I've got a secret, find out what it is." Our Lady said it should have been disclosed at the latest to the people by 1960. It is obvious who is wrong in not disclosing it. It is a test of our Faith today to distinguish the Pope as man and the Pope in his official capacity.

So let us look at these two factors; consecration and reparation. Our Lady promises that when a sufficient number are living lives of consecration, then the Pope will be overwhelmingly graced into obeying God's ecclesial command to consecrate Russia and to declare (and perform) a day of reparation, a season of reparation. Once he does this we will no longer be living under what could be called the Curse of Fatima. We will be living under the blessing of Fatima. We will have a new Zeitgeist, a new spiritual atmosphere. It is up to us. If a sufficient number of us were leading consecrated lives then the Pope would be graced. Why personal consecration? Because we are still individuals no matter how much the liberal Church talks about "community". If I go to Hell and you go to Heaven, your Heaven is not diminished by my being in Hell. We are still individuals. The first and main purpose of consecration is to save our souls from Hell and then to save the souls of others from Hell. That is what Sister Lucy has said. She said that her mission is not to indicate to the world the punishments which are certain to come if the world does not pray and do penance beforehand. She says her mission is to indicate to everyone the imminent danger we are in of losing our souls for all of eternity. It is good to remember this; because of your actions or lack of actions, because of my actions or lack of actions, souls will be forever in Hell or forever in Heaven.

Each of our lives is of infinite and eternal importance. So we consecrate to save others from Hell. St. Paul writes I, "... fill up those things that are wanting of the sufferings of Christ, in my flesh, for His Body, which is the Church." (Col. 1:24)

Consecration Defined

What is consecration? The liberal movement within the Church (even in the highest ranks) trivializes and trashes the word "consecration" to mean merely an "entrustment". This is passive. In truth, consecration is active. It means to sacrifice, to die with Christ and to die to the gods that we worship today in the West. All the world cares about is "the opinion of other people". In the liberal Church in America, all they care about is what other people think. That's why I say never forget the First Commandment. Father Gruner lives in such a way that the First Commandment is primary in his life, and so do a lot of people involved with the Fatima Message. Consecration means first of all to die with Christ, to die to the flesh of the world. To die. To die. Yet we try to get out of it. One way we try to escape it is by bringing in a fifteenth station, The Resurrection. This is not fitting. We are living the Crucifixion now, not the fifteenth station. Now we are here to die with Christ. Woe to you who add to the Bible, the pains of Hell will be added to you. Woe to you who take away from the Bible, you will be taken away from the Book of Life. That is the way the Holy Bible ends. Consecration is more than entrustment. It is a dying with Christ.

Then the question comes up, why consecrate to the Immaculate Heart of Mary? It is partly because historically, humanity rejected the Sacred Heart. God has now offered us His Blessed Mother for mankind. It has been said that the last two devotions will be the Consecration of the Immaculate Heart and the Holy Rosary.

As we consecrate to Mary we consecrate to Christ. This is because our Blessed Virgin Mary is totally transparent to Divinity. We all know that God is love and His love is infinite. He cannot exercise His love with you and I because even though we might say, "Pray for us sinners", we don't mean it. That's why God cannot be manifested in us. But in the Blessed Virgin Mary, He has nothing to impede His love, nothing. She is totally receptive to God. Totally without reserve. One might say She is "divinely" feminine towards God.

The liberals invent new terms, so I invent new terms. Why? It jogs us a little bit. When you invent a new term it makes you think a little bit more about the fundamental truth that the term expresses. I am not denying anything in Catholic teaching. I am just putting a little different phraseology to help us. The liberals do it to hurt us. I do it to help.

In the Greek it says, "Hail Mary, the Channel of Grace". Look in the Greek, it's an emphatic channel, the one and only channel of all graces. She is so receptive to Divinity that real love is completely fulfilled in Her. That is Her essence. That's why She came to Lourdes — to prepare for Fatima. "I am the Immaculate Conception", She said at Lourdes. That is Her identity. As the great Fulton Sheen said, "We used to celebrate the Feast of the Immaculate Conception, now the theologians tell us that we are all immaculately conceived." What demonic pride!

Behold the slave of God, behold the handmaid. Behold the total abject slave of God. The one who is totally receptive, totally feminine, as in "divinely" feminine towards God. Who knows what a handmaid is? I have not met a handmaid in the last twenty years. So Our Lady begins there, "Behold the handmaid of God ..." the perfect slave, the perfectly "divinely" feminine one. In Scripture, during the wedding at Cana, Our Lady said, "Do as He tells you to do," and there we see the "divinely" feminine and what we might call the "divinely" masculine. In other words, once we are totally open to God then we ought to do what God wants us to do. We pray, then we go into the "laboratory", so to speak, and carry out what we have prayed about. We do as God wants us to do. That is what devotion to the Blessed Virgin Mary means. She is "divinely" feminine and totally open to Almighty God.

Christ is the source of salvation. The Blessed Virgin Mary is the fountain through which the source comes to us. She is the channel. The Fatima Message says that God wants both Hearts to be next to each other, to be the focus of man's attention. The Sacred Heart and the Immaculate Heart of Mary. Salvation comes from Jesus through Mary. To any Protestant who objects to this, just point to Colossians 1:24. I ... "fill up those things that are wanting of the sufferings of Christ in my flesh, for His Body which is the Church." It is a beautiful phrase on which to meditate once you get its right meaning.

Another reason to consecrate to the Blessed Virgin in our time is to be part of Mary's Remnant. Chapters 8 through 13 of the Apocalypse is what the Third Revelation concerns. Look at chapter 12, it describes Mary's Remnant. They have overcome by the Blood of the Lamb. By their testimony they obey God's Commandments. They have the testimony of Christ. They adhere to it. In brief, that is what Chapter 12 contains. It describes the Blessed Virgin Mary's Remnant in these end times. In other words, we are totally dedicated to the truth, the fullness of truth in the Roman Catholic Church, through which we will conquer.

The Hierarchy's Rights and Responsibilities

There is a saying in America, "I have my rights". It is seldom pointed out that to have "rights" also means to have "responsibilities". To consecrate someone or something to God is to offer that person or those people to God as His possession, acknowledging that He has supreme dominion over them. How can the Pope and bishops consecrate Russia and the Russian people to God? What right do they have? This Consecration can only be made by those responsible for the eternal salvation of peoples' souls. Who is responsible? The Catholic Church and only the Catholic Church. "Outside the Church there is no salvation." The Message of Fatima is totally Catholic. Who is responsible? You are responsible, the Pope and the bishops. Because of the Catholic hierarchy's responsibilities, they are the ones who have the right to make the Consecration.

The Russian Orthodox Bishops may have the correct sacramental system but they are in heresy. They don't believe in the Immaculate Conception. That's why Our Lady says "Consecrate Russia to the Immaculate Heart of Mary". The Russian Orthodox could not do it. They would have to renounce their religion and become Catholics. You the bishops, and the Pope, are responsible for their salvation, therefore you can consecrate them. My mother was 100% German. She consecrated me. She said, "God give me a boy and I will raise him and I will give him to You when he has grown." Did she have a right to do this? Who is going to stop a German? As bishops, you have the right. As Pope, he has the right. That is your function whether you like it or not.

Consecrate, then Watch the Results

I'm an ex-Jesuit. I've made lots of Ignatian retreats. Ignatius always led you to a decision in the retreat. So in the spirit of an Ignatian retreat, I propose that it is decision time. You, as bishops, can consecrate your nation to the Immaculate Heart of Mary. Then sit back and watch the results. You will be surprised. If you can do this within your nations maybe the fire will catch. Maybe it would go to the top and the Pope will do it. Are you not responsible for the souls of the nation in which you live? Or do you take the viewpoint of the prophet who sat on the hill and was glad that the people were punished?

It is no wonder the Sacred Heart and the Immaculate Heart of Mary grieve. According to a recent survey, eighty percent of the faithful under fifty do not believe in the Holy Eucharist as a Catholic should believe. That is the latest poll and it is the greatest disgrace of the American bishops. This decline in belief must be attributed to the fact that we introduced the people to Communion in the hand. We had to brainwash them into this practice. If it ever existed in the past, the Church corrected it and removed it. We brought the people back into the practice. We are progressing backwards. It is a forced progression. I have been trained as a scientist. I gave these progressives time to experiment, twenty years. The results are in. The person who vacuums the church has to vacuum up the Sacred Hosts. The last church that I was in I had to stop three people within two Masses from taking home the Sacred Host that was in their hand. The results are in. Even if it only happened once in one diocese in one month, Jesus Christ is too important for Him to be treated that way.

So educate your clergy and prepare for the consecration of your nation. Educate yourself and the clergy about the Fatima Message, then start with devotion to the Immaculate Heart of Mary. It still surprises me how people are devoted to the statue of Mary. It brings them to the Blessed Virgin. I am not that type. I have gone through twenty, thirty years of Jesuit training. Nevertheless, when I was in Los Angeles with Father Gruner, my talk was delayed for about ten minutes while the people came up to reverence the statue. It is amazing the power this statue has.

A good friend of mine decided to home-school her little children because she cared about their salvation.

She refused to continue to send them to the establishment Catholic schools. She had already tried two and realized that there was no hope. The day she started home-schooling her statue wept. She called me up and said, "My statue is weeping, what do I do?" I told her to let it weep. It is a sign from God that He approves of what she is doing.

The Blessed Virgin Mary is saying "please get My message out." Even Her statues weep. Try to arrange that each parish has a statue along with devotion to Our Lady of Fatima. It is a good place to start. From there move on to a procession, as did the Bishop of India. Moslems converted as a result. For forty years I couldn't convert one. But somehow by the statue going through the streets, the people seeing the outward display of reverence and the Holy Spirit working through all of this, converts were made according to God's Holy Will. I don't know why, I cannot explain it. It is a puzzle, but it is a fact. Somehow devotion to the Immaculate Heart of Mary is expressed concretely through the use of our statue.

A Realistic Plan for the Consecration of Your Nation

I suggest very strongly that you increase the devotion to the Rosary, to the statue, to processions, then gradually and eventually, once the people are prepared, consecrate your nation to the Immaculate Heart of Mary. The Bishops of Portugal were so devoted to the Immaculate Heart of Mary that according to Sister Lucy, in 1940 God gave the proof of the authenticity of His request. Due to the bishops' consecration of Portugal, to the Immaculate Heart of Mary, God gave His Mercy and special protection. Portugal, as you realize, was spared the horrors of World War II. They suffered but they didn't suffer like other nations. Hitler somehow changed his mind from going into Portugal. We will never know what goes on in the minds and hearts of human beings, but God is in control. God says be devoted to the Immaculate Heart of Mary and consecrate your nation. It worked in Portugal. All of this is in line with the ambiguous parts of the Second Vatican Council in which it teaches that the task of teaching, governing and sanctifying is imposed by the Episcopal Consecration. You are responsible for the people in your diocese and in your nation.

Another thing about Consecration, it leads right to reparation. Just like the Old Testament leads to the New Testament. Consecration leads to reparation. When you consecrate somebody, you have to be consecrated. The Pope in his March 25, 1984, Consecration of the World quoted Scripture. He said, "For their sake, I consecrate myself so they may be consecrated." That is from the Holy Bible. Consecration leads right into reparation. Let us try to get a general view of reparation.

Even Non-Catholics Understand Reparation

In my book *The Awesome Fatima Consecrations* I pointed out that Abraham Lincoln, though not a Catholic, made a proclamation of a day of reparation and consecration. Someone wrote to me with the objection that "Abraham Lincoln went to a seance". I don't know what this reader wanted me to conclude, so I wrote back saying, "If Abraham Lincoln, as wicked as he was, made an act of consecration, how much more shamed are our bishops?" Lincoln, at least, believed in reparation — the little faith that he had shames the total faith that we should possess.

Lincoln said: "It is the duty of nations, as of men, to owe their dependence upon the power of God, to confess their sins with assured hope that genuine repentance will lead to mercy and pardon. To recognize a sublime truth announced in Holy Scripture and proven in history that those nations only are blessed who's God is the Lord. We justly fear that the awful calamity of Civil War which now desolates our land may be but a punishment inflicted upon us for our sins. To pray for forgiveness, we declare a day of National Humiliation, Fasting and Prayer. We do this in the hope, authorized by the Divine teachings, that the united cry of the nation will be heard on high, and answered with blessings, no less than the pardon of our national sins, and restoration of our now divided and suffering country to its former happy condition of unity and peace."

That could apply to our situation today, just change the words a little. The restoration of our now divided and suffering Church may be returned to its former happy condition of unity, peace and prosperity. We are suffering in the United States of America and the West. Do not imitate us. I have stacks of surveys. They all prove that the Church in the United States is in a state of corruption, infidelity and decay.

An article in *30 Days* Magazine, 1992, issue no. 4 says that our times demand that we should stand and confess self-criticism. We should retract, we should denounce ourselves of the past. It is time for a different attitude, a new "psych-geist". It is time for a spirit of reparation that prevails around a whole nation. Instead, the liberals trivialize, trash, cover-up and dilute the Fatima Message so that they can live with it peacefully.

And what does reparation mean? Go to the old Latin text which was used when Sister Lucy received the word, May 5, the Feast of St. Pius V. It says "God, who, to conquer the enemies of the Church and to repair the Divine cult, raised up the great St. Pius V..." Would to

God we had another Pope who would restore the Divine Liturgy to what it should be, God-directed, not man-directed. The *Novus Ordo* English liturgy begins with the priest saying "good-morning", and if the people don't respond, the priest says "I said good morning". This is not God-directed. That is why the priest is facing the people. If you really understand the theology behind the Mass, why not have both the people and the priest, as mediator of the people, facing the same direction, towards God, during the Holy Sacrifice. The modern liturgists are so conscious of symbolism but they miss the essentials. So to repair, in this sense, means to restore to what once was. Even Abraham Lincoln knew that.

Widespread Unbelief

You have to see the mess the Church is in. What can be more insulting to Jesus than that 80% of His alleged Catholics in the United States of America under 50 don't even believe in His Presence as the Church defines it? Universal salvation is the most abominable heresy and it is prevalent in the Catholic Church today. Its form is false ecumenism and the acceptance of the idea that one religion is as good as another. This is total heresy. *Extra Ecclesium Nulla Salus* means outside the Church there is no salvation. It means that only the Catholic Church is the one true Church. That is why Father Gruner has the gift of suffering with Jesus and Mary. But if you don't know reality, how can you suffer with them? If you're one of these liberal optimists, then there's no problem. Everything is wonderful. You never go to the second phase of reparation, to grieve with the Sacred Heart and the Immaculate Heart of Mary. Until you know the problem, you cannot be part of the answer. It is a great grace and if you don't have it, pray that you may get it. That is why the statues weep. They don't cry, as Father Gruner pointed out. They don't smile. They weep. Do you want to join the Blessed Virgin Mary in reparation or not? Do you have the grace? You cannot do it unless you are graced, and you can't be graced unless you use your intellect to realize and confess that the Church is in crisis, because grace builds on nature.

Why did Mary come? She did not come to tell the children that they were doing great, and that the only mistake a person makes is to "think" they made a mistake. This type of talk is the liberal line I learned while going through the Jesuits' Rogerian non-directive approach. Our Lady did not say you have to be sensitive. She said that you have to be sensitive to sin.

Mary's nature is sinless, therefore the only thing that can grieve Her is sin. Sin is totally alien to Her, yet She loves us as a mother and She grieves, She grieves. It's sort of a mystery, how Mary in Heaven can still visit earth and grieve. It is similar to the mystery of how Jesus could be God, the Second Person of the Blessed Trinity, and yet suffer in His Humanity.

The most important aspect of Our Lady's call for reparation is to act on it. Sister Lucy once asked Francisco, "What do you like better, to console Our Lord or to convert sinners so that less will go to Hell"? He answered, "I would rather console Our Lord. Didn't you notice how sad Our Lady was last month, when She said that people must not offend Our Lord anymore, for He is already too much offended?" Sister Lucy also recalled that Jacinta would sometimes kiss and embrace the crucifix exclaiming "O my Jesus, I love You and I want to suffer very much for love of You". You either have the grace, or you don't have the grace, but the first step is to understand the problem. The little children were given a tremendous grace to understand the problem, they were shown a vision of Hell to see the suffering of the condemned. They understood the problem.

You are the Hope of the Church

How important it is to consecrate your nation. On June 12, 1941, Christ complained about the coldness and laxity of the clergy in Spain, both secular and regular, and the remedy was proposed. He said, "Make it known to the Archbishop of Valladolid that I ardently desire the bishops to meet in a retreat to arrange among themselves and determine in common accord, the means to be employed for the reform of the Christian people". Reparation, reparation, reparation. That is a major theme right beside consecration. Consecrate, repair, consecrate, repair.

To paraphrase T.S. Eliot, there is something terribly wrong in the Church's leaders or there is something essentially wrong with Christ's One and Only Church, and that would be too frightening, that would be too frightening, that Christ's One and Only essential Church is wrong. So I'd rather believe that there is something wrong, terribly wrong, with the reigning theologians and alleged experts who run the Church through the Pope, bishops, priests and lesser bureaucrats. (God help you either to admit there is something wrong with the existential Church, or you'll have to conclude that God's Church is wrong and that can never be.)

You are the hope of the Church. If anybody is going to respond on a national level, you will, because you went through a lot of hardship to come here and stay here and God will bless you.

Part III
The
"Divine
Impatience"

Chapter 1

The "Divine Impatience"

by Father Nicholas Gruner

Mary is the spiritual Mother of man. As the Second Vatican Council said, and I'm fond of quoting, the Blessed Virgin is our Mother, not only because She gives us a good example, She is our Mother because She has generated us into the life of sanctifying grace. Just as our natural mother is the one who has generated us into natural life, so our spiritual Mother generates us into supernatural life. The Council text used the Latin word *generavit* which means "She has generated". This Latin word and its meaning points out the real basis for why She is called and is truly our Mother.

The admonition of Tobias to his son said, "Remember the pains that your mother endured in giving you birth". Certainly those words apply to our natural mother. We should respect her and remember her for that and be grateful. But much more so must we be grateful to our spiritual Mother for enduring the pains that She endured in giving us spiritual birth at the foot of the Cross.

When She gave birth to Christ, Our Lord, it was a virginal birth, as our Faith tells us. It is a solemn definition of Church teaching that Mary is a virgin, before, during, and after the birth of Our Lord. She suffered no pain in giving Him birth. But in giving birth to us, She suffered more pain than all the martyrs together. That is why She is called the Queen of the Martyrs — She suffered seeing Her Son die on the Cross.

As Pope Pius XII points out, the Eternal Father would not have allowed Our Lord to be crucified had not the Blessed Virgin Mary given Her free consent and given up Her rights as Mother over Her Son.

When the Blessed Virgin accepted to become the Mother of the Savior, She knew the prophecies of Isaiah. She knew that Her Son would be the Suffering Servant. She knew as His Mother that She would be the Sorrowful Mother. But She accepted this vocation willingly and freely, most of all, because of Her love of God, but also because of Her love for each one of us. That is why we must be grateful and not forget the pains that She endured in giving birth to us.

The Prophet Elias
on Mount Carmel

St. Louis de Montfort and St. Augustine tell us that each of us is carried spiritually in the womb of the Blessed Virgin. We are born of Her only when we enter into eternal life. That is why we wear the Scapular of Our Lady of Mount Carmel. The Scapular as you know goes back to the time of Elias in the Old Testament. Elias was a Prophet. He had a very special devotion to the Blessed Virgin. It came about that he prayed for there to be a drought because the people were not listening to God. So he prayed for there to be no rain. For three and a half years there was no rain and there was great famine in the land. Then Elias prayed that there be rain. He was praying on Mount Carmel. Six times he prayed that God would send rain and six times he sent his assistant down the mountainside to see if any rain was coming. He would go down to the sea and there would be no rain. Six times his assistant came back with the same message. Then Elias prayed the seventh time. This time when his assistant, Achab, went down the mountainside a little cloud came out of the sea in the shape of a foot. This cloud grew and grew until it covered the whole land. It was from this cloud that rain fell on the parched land. Elias understood that through this cloud, in the shape of a foot, God was telling him something, that this cloud represented the Woman of Genesis, the Woman who would crush the serpent's head with Her foot. So Elias founded on Mount Carmel a group of hermits, to prepare for the coming of Christ, to prepare for the coming of Our Lord's Mother.

So it was to the successors of Elias and his hermits, the Carmelite Fathers, particularly, that She came in 1251, to St. Simon Stock, and touched his mantle. The same mantle such as Elias wore, one that was worn over the shoulders, down to the knees in front and in back. She touched his mantle and She said, "Whosoever dies clothed in this shall not suffer eternal fire."

Now, this mantle of the Carmelites symbolizes Our Lady's spiritual maternity. Because the mantle is worn over the shoulder, therefore the mantle of Our Lady covers all Her children in Her spiritual womb. So we entrust ourselves to Her Immaculate Heart, as Pope Pius XII tells us to do. The Scapular of Mount Carmel is the sign of our personal consecration to the Immaculate Heart of Mary. Our Lady promises us that it will protect us from danger, that it will be a sign of peace and a pledge of salvation, that whoever dies wearing this Scapular will not suffer eternal fire.

The Fathers and Doctors of the Church have commented on that passage in scripture about Elias, and they tell us that cloud represents the Blessed Virgin for two reasons. Besides representing the foot that crushes the serpent's head, the cloud was a fresh-water cloud, rising out of the salt-water sea, representing the Immaculate Conception of the Blessed Virgin. From sinful humanity — represented by the salt water — will arise the fresh-water cloud, — without salt — representing She who is without sin. Secondly, it represents Mary,

Mediatrix of All Graces, because it was from the one cloud that rain fell on the sin-parched soil of humanity and that all graces come to us through the Blessed Virgin Mary.

Mediatrix of All Graces

As Pope Leo XIII told us — all graces come to us from God, through the Sacred Humanity of Jesus Christ, through the hands of the Blessed Virgin Mary. It is this great dogmatic truth that God wants everyone, everywhere, to understand. That is why He has brought the world and the Church to this crisis in history. We are in the present crisis because of our sins. But even our sins serve God. God has brought us to this crisis in order to dramatically, much more dramatically than any media event could do, glorify the Blessed Virgin Mary so that people will realize that peace and grace and mercy come through Her.

We are saved through the Blood of Christ. But if the Blessed Virgin had not said, "Yes" to God then Jesus would not have become man and could not have offered His life on the Cross for us. Our salvation depended on Her free consent. That free consent was not only given at the Annunciation but continued up to and included the Crucifixion and Death of Our Lord. Since She was faithful in these few things in this life, and these few things God entrusted Her with in this life are more than all of us together will ever be entrusted with here or hereafter. She has been set over many now that She is in Heaven. Since She refused Our Lord and God the Father nothing, not even the death of Her Son, nothing is refused to Her prayer, now that She is in Heaven.

It is important for us to realize what St. Augustine teaches us, that there are certain graces, certain favors that God in His great love wants to give us. He also recognizes we do not deserve them and that in our weakness we will become proud, thinking somehow that we did it, whether by prayers or sacrifices or whatever. God has reserved certain graces and certain favors only to the intercession and the merits of the Saints. Jacinta said, "God has entrusted the peace of the world to the Immaculate Heart of Mary," that is why peace will not come about any other way except through the plan God has revealed to us at Fatima. That is why the Blessed Virgin said to us, "Only I can help you."

In a certain sense, under Our Lady in turn, only you the bishops, and the Holy Father, can help us. We will not have peace in any other way. Millions of souls will be lost except through your co-operation with Our Lady's plan, that God has outlined and indicated. It is definite, He will not change His mind.

In some prophecies we know that God can "change His mind." One king was told he would die within a day or so. He turned to the wall and cried and prayed to God. As the prophet was walking out the door, God spoke to him again and said, "Go back and tell him I have heard his prayer and I extend his life by 15 years."

Some prophecies are conditional, other prophecies absolute. In the Message of Fatima it is very clear from the context of the words of Our Lady that this is an absolute promise with an absolute condition. She says, "Only I can help you." She also says, "In the end, My Immaculate Heart will triumph, the Holy Father will consecrate Russia to Me, Russia will be converted and a period of peace will be given to mankind." She had predicted the final triumph. But not just the triumph. She has also predicted the manner of the final triumph.

It is important for us to ask Our Lady, Who is the Seat of Wisdom, the Mother of Good Counsel, to guide us and to explain these things to us. I am sure She will.

She has already helped us.

Though it has not been defined, I believe it is definable that Mary is the Mediatrix of all Graces. For those who are aware of this teaching of the Ordinary and Universal Magisterium, it is binding in Faith. As the First Vatican Council teaches, we are not bound to believe only what the Extraordinary Magisterium has solemnly defined and taught but also what the Ordinary and Universal Magisterium of the Church has taught.

It is sufficiently clear in the teaching of Pope Leo XIII as well as popes after him that the Blessed Virgin Mary is the Mediatrix of all Graces. It is the practical results that flow from this doctrine that God wants the faithful to recognize. That is why when Sister Lucy asked the Lord why He would not bring peace to the world and convert Russia without the Act of Consecration, Our Lord answered, "Because I want My whole Church to recognize that Consecration."

Some Fatima commentaries translate that as, "I want My whole Church to recognize that conversion." Either way it means the same thing ultimately — "I want My whole Church to recognize that Consecration as a triumph of the Immaculate Heart of Mary, thereby placing devotion to My Mother's Immaculate Heart beside devotion to My Sacred Heart."

It is God Himself
Who has Asked

Sister Lucy wrote this answer to her confessor who had asked her the question, "Is it convenient to insist on the Consecration?" and Sister Lucy replied by saying, "I answer as I have in the past," and she said, "Not long ago I asked Our Lord about this," and went on to give Our Lord's answer. I understand her answer to mean, "Yes, it is convenient to insist."

I might add, on my own, it is necessary to insist. The Second Vatican Council teaches us in paragraph 37 of *Lumen Gentium* the Faithful have a right and sometimes a duty to bring to the attention of their sacred pastors what is necessary for the good of the Church, especially for the salvation of souls. After fifteen years of working in this apostolate and listening to objections, I can still say, in all truth and honesty, there is nothing more important, more urgent, more necessary for the good of the Church than that the Holy Father and the bishops around the world obey the command of the Queen of Heaven, and of God Himself, to consecrate Russia in the manner prescribed. It is Our Lady who said, "The moment has come in which God asks ...", so, although Our Lady spoke the words, it is truly God Himself who is making the request.

The request was given at the moment Sister Lucy was receiving the solemn vision of the Most Holy Trinity. In mystical communication it is not only the words but also the understanding that is communicated. If at the same time that Sister Lucy was receiving these words she was given to understand aspects of the mystery of the Most Holy Trinity, surely it is not asking too much to believe that the Holy Trinity could also communicate the meaning of these words that Our Lady spoke into her heart.

For 60 years Sister Lucy is publicly on record, from 1929 to 1989, without fear of contradiction of anyone. There were no fake letters circulating before 1989. There were no personal witnesses to Sister Lucy speaking, nor friends like her niece Maria do Fetal, nor her good friend Mrs. Pestana, for that matter, who even claimed that Sister Lucy said the Consecration was done, with one basic exception. That exception was what Father Kramer in his articles refers to as "the bogus interview". They did not have the courage to give us the name of the interviewer who was supposed to have spoken to Sister Lucy on May 13, 1982. But we made such ridicule of the affair that the perpetrators of the hoax backed off and never tried it again. Except for "the bogus interview" no one ever claimed that Sister Lucy contradicted what she had been saying for the last sixty years.

There are people who tell us, even some of those who are in agreement with me on many points, that the testimony of Sister Lucy is not important, that after all, she should just be considered someone who repeated what was said and that was the end of that. I think they are forgetting what Our Lady said to her on June 13, 1917. When Our Lady opened Her hands on that day the light from Her hands fell on the three children as it had fallen on them in the same way on May 13, but this time it was different because the light from one hand fell on Lucy and then went down to the earth, whereas the light from the other hand fell on Jacinta and Francisco and then went up to Heaven. The children understood this light, and Our Lady's words confirmed it. She said, "I will soon come to take Francisco and Jacinta to Heaven but God wishes to leave you longer on earth, in order to make known devotion to My Immaculate Heart."

Lucy was sad at this because she too wanted to go to Heaven and she didn't want to be left without the friendship of her two cousins, Jacinta and Francisco. Our Lady looked at her and said. "You are sad, My child. Do not be sad. My Immaculate Heart will be your comfort. My Immaculate Heart will be your refuge and the way that leads you to God."

It is a very consoling thought that is contained in these words of Our Lady. As Sister Lucy tells us, these words were not only addressed to herself but to all those who are dedicated to the Immaculate Heart of Mary.

God wished to leave her, Lucy, some time longer on earth to make known devotion to the Immaculate Heart of Mary. That vocation she has fulfilled by receiving the request of the Five First Saturdays. On July 13, the Blessed Virgin said, referring to the four chastisements of hunger, war, persecution of the Church and persecution of the Holy Father, "To prevent this I shall come to ask for the Communion of Reparation on the Five First Saturdays and for the Consecration of Russia."

God used Sister Lucy further by coming back to her on December 10, 1925, again to ask for the Communion of Reparation. Sister Lucy was in Pontevedra, a novice in the Dorothean Sisters. She was praying in her room when Our Lady appeared with the Child Jesus. The Child Jesus was about 12 years old and He was standing on a cloud. The Blessed Virgin's Immaculate Heart was circled with thorns. It did not have a sword but thorns surrounding it. The Child Jesus spoke first and said, "Behold the Heart of your Mother surrounded with thorns which ungrateful men put there at every moment by their blasphemies and ingratitude. Do you at least try to console Her by making reparation."

The Blessed Virgin then spoke. She had already placed Her left hand on the shoulder of Sister Lucy, and said, "Announce in My name that I promise to come at the hour of death with all the graces necessary for salvation for those souls that on the first Saturday of five consecutive months go to Confession, receive Holy Communion, keep Me company for fifteen minutes while meditating on the Mysteries of the Rosary and praying five decades of the Rosary with the intention of making reparation to My Immaculate Heart."

The Divine Impatience

That was December 10, 1925. Sister Lucy told her

confessor and told her Mother Superior. Nothing much happened. So on February 15, 1926, just two months and five days later, the Child Jesus came to visit Sister Lucy. It happened in this manner: Sister Lucy was out emptying the garbage in the courtyard when she saw this little boy walking in from the street through the courtyard gate. Lucy recognized him as a boy she had seen some months before and said, "Did you do what I told you?" She was referring to the fact that some months before she had told him to pray the Hail Mary. At that time he would not pray the Hail Mary unless Sister Lucy joined him. Since she had been busy and needed to go about her duties, she asked him if he knew where the Church of St. Mary Major was, it being just around the corner, about a five minute walk from where they stood. The child answered, "Yes, I know where it is". Sister Lucy told him to go there and ask the Blessed Virgin to put Jesus into his heart. So then, the boy had walked off. That had been a few months earlier. She had not seen him again until this day, February 15. So she said to him, "Have you done what I told you? Have you asked the Blessed Virgin to put Jesus into your Heart?" The child then transformed Himself before her eyes and He said, "And what are you doing to promote devotion to My Mother's Immaculate Heart?"

Sister Lucy, of course, recognized Him now. She explained to Him that she had told the Mother Superior and the Mother Superior had replied to her that she could do nothing. The Child Jesus said to Lucy, "Mother Superior is right. By herself she can do nothing but with Me she can do everything." The Child Jesus also explained that the Father Confessor need not concern himself about saying where the message came from, all he had to do was approve the devotion.

Here we see, you might say, the Divine Impatience

over a delay that was just two months and five days in duration. The Child Jesus had come back to rebuke Sister Lucy, Mother Superior and the Father Confessor. So it was also that Our Lord was asked by Sister Lucy on another occasion, at the request of her Confessor, why the five First Saturdays and not nine, like the nine First Fridays, or seven in honor of the Seven Sorrows of Our Lady. Jesus replied, "The answer is simple, My daughter, because of the five major sins that offend the Immaculate Heart of Mary." Then He listed what these sins were and are:

1) those who blaspheme against the Immaculate Conception;

2) those who blaspheme against the perpetual Virginity of His Blessed Mother;

3) those who deny the Spiritual Maternity of the Blessed Virgin Mary over men and Her Maternity over Himself;

4) those who attack the Blessed Virgin in Her sacred images and statues;

5) those who take away from the hearts of children devotion to the Blessed Virgin.

These five sins particularly offend Our Lady and need reparation.

In 1929, on June 13, the Blessed Virgin came back to fulfill Her promise, and to explain more precisely what it was that God wanted. She had promised, "I will come back to ask for the Consecration of Russia." On this occasion, Lucy was praying the prayer taught her by the Angel in 1916. The Angel had come, in 1916, to ask for prayers of reparation to the Sacred Heart of Jesus and the Immaculate Heart of Mary for crimes against the Blessed Sacrament. Sister Lucy was praying the prayer of the Angel on the night of June 12 to 13. She had permission from her superiors to follow the prayers of St. Margaret Mary Alacoque, that is, prayers of reparation to the Sacred Heart on each Thursday of the month. As she was praying, the chapel which had been all in darkness except for the vigil light, was lit by a supernatural light. As she looked up, she saw Our Lady standing on a cloud. Beside Her, on the Cross, was Her Son, Jesus, and over His head was the Holy Spirit. Above God the Son, and God the Holy Spirit, was God the Father in the form of an older man. The Eucharist, the Host, came from the wound in the side of Our Lord. From the Host fell drops of blood into the chalice which was suspended in the air underneath the Host. All this was under His right arm. Under His left arm were the words in waterlike form, "Grace and Mercy". Lucy tells us that at this time she was given to understand aspects of the Mystery of the Most Holy Trinity that it is not permitted for her to speak about or reveal.

Our Lady had the Rosary in one hand and Her Immaculate Heart again circled with thorns in the other. The Blessed Virgin said, "The moment has come in which God asks the Holy Father to make, and to command all the Catholic Bishops of the world to make, the Consecration of Russia to My Immaculate Heart promising to save Russia by this means. There are so many sins which the justice of God condemns to Hell committed against Me that I have come to ask reparation."

Here we see the "vengeance" of the Blessed Virgin. She comes to ask for our prayers and reparation for the very people who offended Her. For the very people who encircled Her Heart with thorns.

Just two years and two months later, in August of 1931, we again encounter the Divine Impatience. Lucy was in Rianjo and Jesus spoke to her saying, "Make it known to My ministers, given that they follow the example of the King of France in delaying the execution of My command, like him, they will follow him into misfortune. They will repent of this, then they will do it, but it will be late."

Father Trinchard points out in his book that if there is to be an act of repentance for delaying, it implies there was some guilt for not complying earlier.

The Bishops Must Intervene

As a bishop, St. Augustine said, "With you, I am a Christian and I rejoice in it. For you, I am a bishop and I tremble for it." The responsibility of the bishops is indeed great before God and before man. We have prayed many Rosaries for you as we also pray for the Holy Father. We stopped counting after we collected twelve million Rosaries for the Holy Father to make this act of Consecration. We have collected many Communions and other acts of piety from the faithful around the world. So we feel heartfelt gratitude that you are our bishops, that you have taken this responsibility and we feel heartfelt gratitude that the Holy Father has accepted the cross of being the Pope. At the same time we realize our own duty. As Jesus Himself has told us, "Pray, pray, pray a great deal for the Holy Father. He will do it but it will be late."

From reading both Deirdre Manifold, *Fatima and the Great Conspiracy* and Ralph Epperson, *The New World Order*, as well as the books of Father Fahey, I can see that today we are indeed surrounded. We are indeed in great need of the intervention of the bishops. All of us — from the Holy Father to the bishops to the priests to the lay people — are all in the same boat. We know it is only you, together with the Holy Father, who can save the ship. That is why when Sister Lucy was asked, "Is it convenient to insist?" that she answered the way she did, "It is indeed convenient to insist."

A lot has happened since that time. One of the problems today is that there is a lot of false information out there. I know that some of you have questions about it. Also, there is a lot of false theology out there. I remember when I was studying Sacred Scripture in my second year theology, I wondered why God permitted St. Peter and St. Paul to have a dispute. I said, "this is not right. After all, how can we defend ourselves against the Protestants who attack the Papacy when they have that Scripture passage falling right into their hands?" Of course, I did not understand the passage as well as I should have. I'm afraid that there are many popular writers with regards to the Message of Fatima who have the same sense of false interpretation of the Pope and are not familiar with St. Paul's letter to the Galatians or to the Acts of the Apostles in regards to St. Peter's visit to Antioch.

St. Peter, as you know, on that occasion had just defined in the Council of Jerusalem, the First Council of the Church, that it was indeed of Faith that to be saved you did not need to be circumcised. What was necessary was obedience to the law of God, that is, the Ten Commandments, and obedience to the law of Christ. But the ceremonial law of Moses was no longer necessary. In fact, St. Thomas Aquinas proves that to follow the ceremonial Law of Moses would be an act of heresy because those Sacraments of the Old Testament referred to the future coming of Christ. To insist on those Sacraments of the Old Law today would be a denial that Christ has actually come.

St. Peter never contradicted the truth that he had proclaimed in Jerusalem but he acted as if he did. St. Peter did not eat with non-circumcised Catholics and ate only with those Catholics who had also been circumcised. His action most likely was done, as Scripture scholars tell us, because he wanted peace in the community, a very wholesome motive. But his action also gave rise to the heretical impression that you needed to be circumcised in order to be saved. So, St. Paul, seeing what was happening, publicly rebuked St. Peter to his face. He said, "you are not standing in the truth." St. Peter, to his credit, recognized the truth of what St. Paul was saying and changed his manner of acting. Now that is in Sacred Scripture.

Three Kinds of Scandal

To some Catholics today, as it was at one time, it was a scandal. As Scripture tells us, and again, St. Louis de Montfort teaches, there are three kinds of scandal. There is the scandal which is, simply speaking, scandal, that is, if I were to steal a thousand dollars, and someone saw me do it and they said, well, if Father Gruner can do it, I can do it too, I would have scandalized someone. Of course that would be wrong, not only because it is wrong to steal a thousand dollars but also because it is wrong to scandalize someone.

There is a second kind of scandal which is called the scandal of the weak. St. Paul writes about it when he speaks to the Catholics of his time. Now those Catholics were well-informed. They recognized that God created all of creation including animals which, Genesis tells us, is for meat to eat. Therefore, there is nothing wrong with eating meat. Even if some pagans had offered that meat for sacrifice, it is not wrong in itself. However, St. Paul points out that there are those who are weak in their Faith, who are not so well-informed. If they saw you eating meat sacrificed to idols they might get the impression that you agree with idol worship. St. Paul therefore says why lose those souls for the sake of a little meat? You can go hungry, instead of taking what is rightfully yours, if by eating it you thereby scandalize the weak.

Now there is a third kind of scandal which Our Lord Himself attacked. It is called Pharisaical scandal. Our Lord worked miracles on the Sabbath — cured the sick and did other good things. The Pharisees would say to Him, "Do not do that because we are scandalized." Our Lord refused to change His ways. He refused to stop doing the good that must be done because of the evilness of those who were scandalized. The expression in French, *Honni soi qui mal y pense* applies here. "Shame to those who think evil." If someone is scandalized by me doing some good then it shows the evilness of their ways. Rather, I would be wrong to stop doing the good I am doing, or anyone else, for that matter, because someone has Pharisaical scandal. I am afraid that is what we are dealing with, in part, with some of the objections that are raised to our Fatima Consecration Crusade.

Josyp Terelya has spoken to the Holy Father. Josyp tells us that there is nothing preventing the bishops, in their own dioceses, from doing what Father Gruner does to promote the need for the Consecration of Russia. The Holy Father sees this preparation as necessary before he does the Act of Consecration. Whether it is necessary or not is the question but certainly it would be a good thing to promote this Consecration Crusade in your own diocese in your own country, to collect prayers for the Holy Father, as Jesus Himself told Sister Lucy, "Pray, pray, pray a great deal for the Holy Father. He will do it but it will be late."

The Holy Father has shed his blood and has recognized that it was through the intervention of Our Lady of Fatima that his life was saved. The Pope bent over as the first shot was fired at him to kiss a little girl who had an image of Our Lady of Fatima on her blue and white dress. That bullet would have killed him. It is not widely known that the bullets were poisoned. If the bullet didn't kill him, the poison should have. We know that because the two women that were shot with him also suffered the same very strange disease. What is not so very well known, perhaps, is that the poison came not from Russia but from the United States. It points to the fact that the conspiracy, whether you call it Capitalism, Communism or Socialism, has one headquarters. Ultimately it is from Hell. But even on earth it is directed by the same people. They are in league with each other to destroy the Church. As the second Psalm says, "Why have the kings of the earth raged against Christ, against God and His anointed, that is, against God and His Christ?"

We are living in that time when the kings of the earth, for the most part, are fighting against God, Christ and His Church, and the Holy Father. Josyp Terelya also says the reason why the Holy Father does not consecrate Russia is because of the pressure exerted on him to this day by Moscow.

The Holy Father needs our help. He needs above all, our prayers, our sacrifices, and our good will. I hope I continue to be a faithful, loyal son of Pope John Paul II and his successor. But as important and as great as the Holy Father is, we must first of all listen to Our Lady of Fatima.

It is not Wrong to Proclaim the Full Message of Fatima

"They will repent of it and will do it but it will be late." I certainly believe the Holy Father wants to, but even if he didn't want to do it, which I do not believe, it still would not be wrong for us to proclaim publicly the full Fatima Message, which has been approved by the

Church, to explain in simple terms what it means for all of us. The reason it would be wrong for us not to proclaim it is for the same reason that Peter gave to the Sanhedrin when they told him not to speak out in Jesus' name. "Whether it is right in the sight of God to listen to you rather than God, decide for yourselves. For we cannot but speak of what we have seen and heard."

Five Popes — Pius XI, Pius XII, John XXIII, Paul VI and John Paul II — have all approved of the Message, have all encouraged the diffusion of the Message. Two Popes have come here to Fatima. Pope John Paul II has come twice. If there is any confusion about the Message it is because the theologians, *who claim to have the Holy Father for their origin,* claim that the Message is not important or it is mumbo jumbo or it is magic. These words, if they are not blasphemous, border on blasphemy, yet these objections are raised by the very people who claim to be faithful to Our Lady of Fatima.

What is the essential difficulty? Bishop Rego has asked the question, "Why has the Holy Father not come forward to suggest that the Consecration may be done?"

I will tell you a little story I know about the Holy Father when he was Archbishop of Cracow. It is a very simple story and it is a very nice story. Archbishop Wojtyla was asked to lead a procession to Our Lady of Czestochowa. The times were the worst for the Church. At the time, he refused. It's not that he was against the procession in honor of Our Lady of Czestochowa. On the contrary, he didn't feel the moment was opportune for him to lead it. The people nevertheless started the procession. A large crowd joined in. When the procession got to a large enough size, the Archbishop was very pleased to join it himself.

I tell this story because I think it is his style. He doesn't want to be too far ahead of his flock. When he realizes that he has enough support to do what he wants to do then he himself will more than happily join them. Everyone knows his devotion to Our Lady.

Chapter 2

Save Our Children

by Coralie Graham

Nobody Will Help Us

As editor of *The Fatima Crusader* I receive thousands of letters a week and I can tell you people out there are crying. They are not getting Catholic leadership. We, the lay people, have no voice anymore. That is why people are pleading, "Please, lead us. Speak to the bishops. Tell them we're hurting. Our children's souls are going to Hell and nobody will help us."

One lady wrote and said she cries every day because, "When I go to Mass, before Mass I pray the Rosary, and the priest came and yanked the Rosary out of my hand, broke it in the middle of the church and the beads rolled down the aisle."

That's the kind of leadership we are getting. Nobody in a position of authority is stopping it. They go to the bishop and the bishop says, "Well, I'll talk to him." But nothing happens.

Countless people are told, "Don't pray the Rosary in the church; you're disturbing the people." This to a nice little group of ten to fifteen parishioners praying the Rosary before Mass. Not during Mass. Not during any other liturgical events going on. Just very quietly. But still being told, "No. You disturb the people."

What About Our Children

Contraception is a sin, yet they're inviting Protestants into the Catholic schools to show Catholic students all the various contraceptive devices available to them and how to use them. This under the complete approval of the school principals and the bishop. When students themselves questioned this anti-Catholic practice, they were told, "Oh, we're not telling them to use it. We're only showing them how."

A priest in one diocese preaches to his whole congregation that, "None of my congregation is going to Hell because I know you all love God. And if you love God, you cannot commit a mortal sin. Even if you murder someone, you can't go to Hell, because you love God. You have to hate God when you murder someone in order to be condemned to Hell".

I know better. I know that is heretical. I thank God I was taught by the strict Loretto nuns when I grew up. They planted the seed of Faith into my heart so I knew better.

But what about our children? They haven't had the advantage I had to have our full Catholic Faith taught in school, they haven't heard soul-saving sermons from the pulpit. The Church and the school system are no longer teaching them not to sin.

Rather, they are being encouraged to become complacent and sin. They are actually being encouraged to listen to their own unformed conscience rather than take direction from their parents.

They are Being Led to Hell

In school now they are teaching children to respect homosexuals. Not just the person of the homosexual but also their sinful act. They are showing them in class, through films, how to engage in homosexual activity. And they're saying, "You must learn to accept and respect what they are doing."

We all know what God had to say about homosexuality in the Bible. I don't want my children going to a school and being taught by a homosexual teacher who is telling them that it is okay.

I have a beautiful statue at home. It's Our Blessed Mother reaching Her hands out to us with love, giving us the graces we need to be solid in our Faith. She was found in a bushel basket, broken to pieces, thrown out in the garbage. Some nuns glued Her together but were not allowed to keep Her because their half-way house for young girls was partially government funded. They had to take all the crucifixes and statues out of the classrooms or be shut down for lack of funding.

They gave Her to me and I took Her home and painted Her. She was so beautiful and appealing I was determined to put Her back in the church where She belonged. When I offered Her to the priest, he said, "Oh, no, I can't put Her in the church. She doesn't match the wall. She doesn't match the decor."

I also have at home a beautiful set of Stations of the Cross, four feet high, oil on canvas and encased in oak. These were "rescued" along with five foot high statues of St. Anthony and the Sacred Heart of Jesus. And just in time. They were destined for destruction and transportation to the garbage dump.

What the Bishops Can Do to Help

I have heard people say that the consecration of Russia has been done. I have heard others say that the consecration has not been done. There are esteemed bishops and priests on both sides. One side says, "I have asked the Holy Father and he tells me yes." The other side says, "I have asked the Holy Father and he tells me no."

Regarding what the Holy Father really thinks, I believe we should get an absolute authoritative ecclesiastical statement from him to rid the confusion. What we are praying the bishops will do is to ask the Holy Father to make a definitive ecclesiastical pronouncement.

The Message of Fatima says Our Lady will triumph. I cannot say it is a triumph when I see more souls going to Hell than ever before. I would be spouting blasphemy to say this is Her triumph. Her message says there will be peace in the world. Where is there true peace in the world? Some people say Sister Lucy meant "peace" in the "heart". Where is this "peace" of "heart"? In my country, teenagers are killing themselves every day and killing other people with them. How can we say this is Our Lady's triumph?

Our Lady does not lie. Even those who believe the consecration is done have to admit something is wrong.

Millions of Catholics are crying out for help to the bishops. Our Lady told us all, lay people and religious alike, "Only I can help you."

I now say to you bishops, in order to bring about the triumph of Our Lady, only you can help us.

Chapter 3

Steps Needed To Fulfill
The Fatima Message

by Father Nicholas Gruner

I have been accused of repeating myself but at the same time I see that my point has not been understood with regard to this little prayer that Jesus taught. This little prayer that Jesus taught is the context for Our Lord's words to Sister Lucy. But the context is very important. It's also important for us to realize that these are the only two prayers that Jesus taught in the Message of Fatima. You might ask yourselves why it is that only *The Fatima Crusader* repeats these prayers and teaches them to the world? It is not because we are holy. Perhaps it is because we have been too intellectual in our formation. As one bishop said; "You are too well educated." Perhaps that is my cross. But at least I understand these two prayers in their context. I think they are very important and they answer a number of your questions.

Lucy, at that time being 24 years old, was praying for the conversion of Spain, Portugal, Europe, Russia and the world, when Our Lord came and spoke to her. He said, "You please Me very much by praying for the conversion of those countries and you console Me a great deal by asking for the conversion of those poor nations. Ask it also frequently of My Mother by saying: 'Sweet Heart of Mary be the salvation of Russia, Spain, Portugal, Europe and the whole world'."

Ten Just Men

Our Lord was recognizing that we are not here to judge Russia. We are not here to say they are worse than we are. It is not our intention nor our implication to say that. If we have done that, it is only our fault for not knowing how to speak properly. This accusation is made time and again, that somehow or other we are against Russia. Or that we don't know anything else about the Message of Fatima. It is rather that the Message of Fatima has an apex. The Holy Father will not do the consecration of Russia unless a certain number of bishops join him. I compare them to the ten just men. Just as the ten just men would have saved Sodom and Gomorrah if God could have found them. So God will save the world if He can find, proportionally speaking, ten just men. It is through the prayers and sacrifices of those ten just men, whether they be bishops, Pope, priests, or lay people, that will be brought about the grace needed for the Holy Father and the bishops to do the consecration.

It is through the instrumentality of the consecration of Russia that peace will be given to the world, because God wants to glorify His Mother. God wants to glorify you, the bishops. He wants you to be more respected in the world than you've ever been in your lives. He wants to bring about worldwide peace. Not the non-shooting war existing between the United States and Russia for the last forty, fifty years, but positive peace. Not piece-meal attacking of this country, that country, or subjecting to attack this group of people or murdering that group of babies. Peace in its full dimensions around the whole world in every class of society. Peace that the world has never yet seen. It is a vision that is told of in Isaiah. "The lion will lay down with the lamb." We have never seen that. But that is what She promises for the simple act of obedience. And it will not come any other way. I wish it would. My life would be easier. But that's the way it is. That's the simple truth. You can accept it.

You can reject it. You can do what you want with it. Whatever you do you answer to God, not to me. But that is the truth and if I don't tell you the truth, I will have to answer to God. I have done my duty.

The Steps

Consecrate your countries. Consecrate your parishes. Promote the Rosary. Make the Message known. Promote the Scapular, make it understood. Make people aware as much as you can by the force of your arguments, by your example, by grace, by whatever you have at your disposal. Address the Message to persons, to souls, to individuals. Make it understood and loved. Then we will find our ten just men, who will obtain by their prayers, sufferings, sacrifices, this great grace that we do not deserve.

I am fully aware that the Message of Fatima is much more than the Consecration of Russia. But I am also fully aware that it is a part of the Message that has been hidden. It was hidden from me for the first six years of my work. I've worked for fifteen years for Fatima. For the first six years I myself did not know this aspect of the Message. I had nothing else to do but to study the Message of Fatima. Yet for six years I was in darkness about this request. So I can well understand that you did not have the opportunity to understand its central importance.

One of the bishops as I came in said, "Let us do whatever we choose to do, that is what the Church wants." The last bishop spoke about Church History. I find many lessons in Church History. I think if we learned theology only from dogmatic books and we don't put it together with Church History, we can also lose a little bit of the flesh and blood of theology. I like both. To quote Church History early on from the Acts of the Apostles, Chapter 20, St. Paul when he's departing, I believe from Ephesus, is telling the priests and the bishops gathered there, "You will see me no more. I go to Jerusalem and I will be taken prisoner. I want to witness before you today that I have not been afraid to tell you the whole counsel of God. I have hidden nothing from you. I have done what I told Timothy. In other words, I have spoken the Gospel when convenient and inconvenient. Nevertheless from among your own number will arise some who will lead the Faithful after them. Taking them away from Christ."

In so saying he was predicting such would happen from among priests such as Arius, such as Luther. They would take away the Faithful. They would make them fall into Hell with them. And from among the bishops like Nestorius, there would arise others who would take away the Faithful from the Church. In the time of Arius, the Arian Heresy was condemned in the Council of Nicea in 325. It was defined that Jesus Christ is True God, True Man consubstantial with the Father. Equal every way in His Divinity. Yet remember in 336, eleven years later, the Arians succeeded in changing one letter in one word. Our Faith is transmitted by words, whether spoken or written it is transmitted through words. We do not see the unreal, the invisible realities our Faith teaches. But God nevertheless transmits them to us by faith, by preaching, by words. Words are sacred when they carry the Message of God. So when the Arian heretics changed one letter of one word, in a solemn definition of the Church, it caused the renewal of the Arian Heresy. History tells us that as a result of this ruse, ninety percent of the bishops were wrong on this matter. At this time, only three bishops in the whole Catholic Church defended the truth that Jesus Christ is True God and True Man in the full sense of the words as the Council of Nicea defined it. As St. Jerome, Doctor of the Church, tells us, Catholics went to bed one day Catholic and the next day woke up and they were Arian. It wasn't until 381 A.D. that the true doctrine was again preached by all Catholic Bishops. Those are facts of Church history. We have no partisans of Arius or otherwise here. All I am saying is there is a lesson to be learned. The truth, as Cardinal Ratzinger has told us, is not determined by majority rule. The Truth is the Truth. We can stay with the majority. We can stay with the minority. We can be wrong either way. But we must be with the Truth.

With regard to the relationship of the Pope, perhaps you are not aware that the Fifth Lateran Council has defined that, in matters of prophetic revelation, the Pope is the only judge. I am not here to criticize the Holy Father. I'm not here to judge the Holy Father. I hope no one else is either. But we do ask for a judgement on a prophetic revelation. The Message of Fatima has been approved. But as several bishops have noted, there is the question of the interpretation. I agree. It is possible that we can have unity by politics — that is, we can all say, well, let us agree with the majority and then we have this superficial unity. It will not cause real unity by itself. The majority of men can serve a lie for a while without disagreeing among themselves. For the sake of unity, Christ founded His Church on the rock of Peter. And He gave authority to Peter to exercise for the good of the Church. But as long as the question has been left open, and the Holy Father for his own good reasons does not give an authoritative judgement on this, then I cannot be asked to remain silent on the obvious and continued understanding of this Message for the last sixty years and more.

I would very much love for the Holy Father to engage his pastoral Petrine authority, which has been defined by the Fifth Lateran Council, and settle this question. He has a right to do it and we have a need for it. Otherwise history will catch up to us. We will have the annihilation of nations. As to my right to ask for this, it has been defined twice. It was defined as Dogma of the Catholic Church in 1274, at the Council of Lyons, that in matters pertaining to ecclesiastical jurisdiction, everyone, including lay people, have the right to ask for a ruling. That is Catholic Dogma. If you do not believe this, I will tell you where to look it up. If you don't believe it after you realize it's Catholic Teaching, you are not Catholic. That is the nature of Divine Catholic Dogma. It cannot change. Just as the teaching of the Church, outside the Church there is no salvation.

Yesterday I heard a prayer said from the Sanctuary which was heretical. But I said maybe the priest means it another way. Some Father speaking in English, said, "We pray that the Protestants and the Orthodox and the Catholics can receive communion together." Now if he meant that while they were remaining Protestant, remaining Orthodox, remaining Catholic, then that is a heretical prayer. I said maybe he means that the Orthodox convert to Catholic and the Protestants convert to Catholic in which case it would be a Catholic prayer. But I am told he meant it in a heretical sense. The man who spoke to him understood that. But be that as it may, my point is very simply that if you want unity, unity has to be in Truth. If you want to know the truth of the Prophetic Message of Fatima, outside the Pope defining it, which he has a right to do, then it is incumbent upon us to do what the first bishop from the Philippines said, "Why don't we just do the consecration again. This time do it according to the request as it has been commonly understood for the last sixty years, mention Russia and have done with it."

Either way, make a definition and tell us it doesn't mean what it says, or do the consecration the way it was requested. Either way you will have peace and unity. Not doing either one of them, we will still have the prophecies of Our Lady of Fatima and of Our Lord as the consequences of ignoring Her request. We have the right to ask for a definition and the First Vatican Council in 1870 again defined that the Pope has supreme jurisdiction. He also has the right to command the bishops in matters not only for faith and morals but for the good of the Church. Therefore, in keeping with both the Second Vatican Council and First Vatican Council, Our Lady's demand that the Pope command the bishops to consecrate Russia is perfectly within his jurisdiction.

Bishop Arulappa Stresses Need for Collegial Consecration

This letter was sent to the world's bishops along with a copy of Father Paul Trinchard's book *The Awesome Fatima Consecrations*. It is being included in this book as Archbishop Arulappa's letter soundly reinforces the need for the Consecration of Russia and the urgency of the Fatima message.

MOST REVEREND R. ARULAPPA
Archbishop of Madras & Mylapore (Retired)
Our Lady of Light Church, Madras, India

Holy Thursday, 1992

Dear Brother Bishop:

Father Gruner has told me of his admiration for the tremendous love and generosity that you have shown Our Dear Blessed Mother. How gratifying it is for me to hear of such strong devotion to Our Lady of Fatima!

That is why I especially wanted to write you and share my thoughts regarding the enclosed book which Father is sending you as a gift this Easter season.

First off, I would like to say that *The Awesome Fatima Consecrations* is truly a book for our times. The heart of Father Trinchard's main message is fully convincing and scarcely questionable.

While a few comments in the book are perhaps controvertible, this takes nothing away from the great usefulness and good that this book will do if it is widely circulated.

It seems clear to me, as it does to Father Trinchard, that we are actually living in the end-times referred to by Our Lord in Luke 18.8: "But yet the Son of man, when He cometh, shall He find faith on earth?"

It does not require any extraordinary perception to realize that these troubled days of ours are just such times. Where is faith these days? In what nation does it flourish, in what place?

The general apostasy predicted in Holy Scripture is occurring now before our eyes. And, as Father Trinchard shows, what is most unfortunate is that this "smoke of satan" (as Pope Paul VI called it) has not spared even the very heart of the Church!

For several years now, I have been mystified and baffled by the fact that at least three Popes (Pius XII, Paul VI and our present Pontiff, John Paul II) all *partially* obeyed Our Lady by consecrating the world, yet each stopped short before fulfilling the most important part of Her Fatima request, namely the collegial consecration of Russia.

Pope John Paul II himself has even said (after consecrating the world in 1984) that Our Lady was still waiting for the specific consecration of Russia that She asked for at Fatima.

It would seem clear, as Father Trinchard suggests, that some kind of agreement between the Vatican and Moscow continues to stand in the way. Obviously the devil, the most cunning of all creatures, seems to have lured even the Popes into a disastrous situation.

1. Objections to Fatima and the Consecration of Russia

Some of those who object to the Consecration say that because it is a "private revelation" it is not valid. The revelation of the Sacred Heart of Jesus through Saint Margaret Mary was also private, yet it was officially accepted and the Feast of the Sacred Heart and the devotion of the First Fridays were instituted.

Similarly, the revelation of the Immaculate Conception at Lourdes was private, but nevertheless it was used to confirm the dogma which was proclaimed four years earlier. Here too, a Feast was instituted in honor of the apparition of Our Lady at Lourdes.

Why is it then the revelation of the Immaculate Heart of Mary at Fatima is the object of so much doubt and scorn? The only reason seems to be that a conspiracy of demons has somehow succeeded in preventing the fulfillment of Our Lady's Fatima promises.

Interestingly, the revelations of Paray-le-Monial, Lourdes and Fatima are not really "new" revelations at all, but rather confirmations of the revelation made by Christ Himself. They are warnings, pleadings and merciful appeals to live by that first great revelation and the truth revealed through Christ, a truth that can be summed up in the words: Repent, Pray, Do Penance...

There are still others who object to the Consecration on the grounds that it constitutes "interference" in the internal affairs of Russia. Consecration is indeed a very special kind of prayer, but since when does prayer interfere in any negative way?

We must never forget that it was the Mother of God Who made this request. Do we dare believe that She did not know what She Herself was asking for? One can only imagine that the "father of lies" has cleverly blinded the eyes of those who say such things.

When Our Lady asked for the Consecration, She knew that Russia's power would be very great and that it would be capable of using enormous influence, both for good and bad.

Just as obviously, by delaying the fulfillment of this request we have missed a great chance to use that power for good, to use it for conversion and for the peace that Our Lady promised us.

Why is Our Lady so concerned about Russia? Because it is God's Will and because devotion to Her in Russia is so extraordinary, even today. And yet what was and remains "Holy Russia" may well be given up into the enemy's hands because of lack of faith.

2. Why the Immaculate Heart?
And Why Now?

It seems that many of those who complain about the Consecration really object to the loving appeals of the Sacred and Immaculate Hearts. In fact, they reject the warnings which have been given by God for the good of all mankind.

In the final analysis, the campaign against the Consecration is really the last great effort of satan to conquer because he knows that the triumph of the Immaculate Heart means his final defeat.

The question arises why so much insistence on the Immaculate Heart of Mary now?

As Our Lord Himself told Sister Lucy, it is His way of making the Church honor and glorify His Mother! If a son like Jesus chooses to honor and glorify His Mother in these end-times (for having co-operated so richly with Him in the work of redemption), who are we to question Him?

The real problem for the objectors is that they do not want to acknowledge Mary as our Co-Redemptrix and Mediatrix (perhaps because they fear offending those "separated brethren" outside the true Faith).

This is despite the fact that the Second Vatican Council itself acknowledges Our Lady as Advocate, Helper, Benefactress and Mediatrix (Paragraph 62, *The Constitution of the Church*).

One can only wonder why those who swear by Vatican II choose to ignore the words of the Council Fathers when they declare that Mary "in a wholly singular way ... co-operated in Her obedience, faith, hope and burning charity in the work of the Savior in restoring supernatural life to souls."

In the end, we cannot doubt that it is Satan's effort to bring down the glory of Mary — a glory which the Father has not hesitated to bestow upon Her!

3. Help the Pope and Bishops

As incredible as it may seem to you, it is unfortunately very true that many bishops have not taken Fatima seriously. And what a terrible pity it is!

The Queen of Heaven and Earth, the Mother of Mankind (and in a very special way, the Mother of all priests and bishops) pleads and begs for something and still it is not taken seriously.

Yet even at this late date, being the merciful Mother that She is, Our Lady will do everything and anything to save us from total catastrophe!

We should not be surprised or scandalized that so many bishops are not worried. As Father Trinchard shows, neither the Popes nor the bishops are impeccable or infallible in matters of pastoral administration (the Pope's infallibility is restricted to faith and morals alone), hence a mistake in prudential matters is very possible.

While many statements in *The Awesome Fatima Consecrations* will be irksome to those concerned, we must remember that the truth is always irksome, and can we not reasonably expect our bishops to rise above any personal discomfort to please God and Our Lady?

When will the Holy Father and the bishops fulfill Our Lady's request for the Consecration of Russia?

We can only hope and pray that it will be soon. What is truly needed today is a vast worldwide campaign of prayer, asking Almighty God to give the Pope and bishops the graces needed to obey Our Lady of Fatima and consecrate Russia as She asked.

In these circumstances, I think Father Trinchard's book is uniquely valuable. It may also help to open the eyes of many bishops and it is certainly most desirable (even necessary) that it be placed in their hands as soon as possible!

I am certain that Our Lady will bless you so much for any help you can give to get Father Trinchard's book out to all the bishops, priests and other influential people who can do something to get the Consecration of Russia accomplished now!

I invoke God's abundant blessing on you and your family. Please remember that it is never too late to call on Mary's Motherly goodness.

Yours in Our Lady,
Archbishop R. Arulappa

Letters of Encouragement and Gratitude

from Catholic Bishops

to Father Nicholas Gruner

Before the 1992 Conference

"In the name of Cardinal Fiorenzo Angelini, I thank you for the invitation to participate in the Fatima Peace Conference. But unfortunately, the Cardinal is already engaged in a tight program. We will offer the holy sacrifice of the Mass for the spiritual success of this Conference.

   Father José L. Redrado, O.H.
   Secretery to Cardinal Fiorenzo Angelini
   Pontificium Consilium de Apostolatu
   pro Valetudinis Administris,
   VATICAN CITY

"Peace and joy. I am most grateful for your personal invitation to attend THE FATIMA PEACE CONFERENCE to be held from October 8th onwards. You can be sure, Father Gruner, that I support your efforts to consecrate Russia to the Immaculate Heart of Mary as per Her appeal. My prayers and sacrifices are with you for this purpose.

   Please do pray to Our Lady of Fatima for me and for our diocese, as I too shall pray for Her mission and for the success of your work."

   With fraternal good wishes,
   Devotedly Yours,
   Ignatius Minezes
   Bishop of Ajmer-Jaipur, India

"Thank you very much for your recent letter in connection with the Fatima Peace Conference, and by which you invite me to attend.

   It is indeed gratifying that men and women are giving so much of their energy, talent and time to promote peace and to invite all to do the same by seeking the intercession of our Blessed Mother Mary, Mother of Our Lord and of the Church. I am therefore deeply touched by your most kind invitation to me to attend this Conference for Peace."

With every prayerful wish for a successful conference, I remain,

Yours very sincerely in Christ,
Peter Poreku Dery
Archbishop of Tamale, Ghana

"I wish to thank you for your remembrance of me, your kind words, and cordial invitation.

I wish to assure you that I will be present in spirit and in prayer during the observance of the sacred anniversary of the Apparitions at Fatima.

With prayerful good wishes, as I ask Our Lady, the Mother of the Church, and our loving Mother to watch over your many endeavors."

Sincerely yours in Christ,
Cardinal Carberry of St. Louis

"Thank you for the inspiring letter you forwarded to me on the Feast of the Sacred Heart this year.

I am fully convinced that a true devotion to Our Lady of Fatima and the acceptance of its message can stimulate a spiritual life for the good of the Church.

With God's blessing on your apostolate for peace in the world, I remain"

Sincerely yours in Christ,
Ceirano Giovanni
Apostolic Pro-Nuncio
Papua New Guinea

"Replying to your letter about the Fatima Peace Conference, I will let you know that I, in the spirit of the Holy Father John Paul II, will pray for the good success of the above mentioned conference.

Unfortunately I cannot leave the Vatican at the time the conference is being held."

With kind regards and good wishes.
Sincerely,
Bishop Peter Canisuis van Lierde
VICAR GENERAL of Vatican City

Excerpts

"I appreciate all you are doing in this connection and for world peace, and pray that your endeavors will be crowned with success".

Blasco Francisco Collaco
Apostolic Pro-Nuncio to
Madagascar & Maritius

"You are doing a great job indeed when most of us are lying idle".

William D. D'Mello
Bishop of Kawar, South India

"I am convinced that the time has come as you say in your letter, dear Father Gruner, to openly and publicly address the entire issue of Our Lady's request for the Consecration of Russia."

Oscar Andres Rodriguez Maradiaga
Auxiliary Bishop of Tegucigalpa, Honduras

"Again I reconfirm my willingness to join the Holy Father to consecrate Russia if requested by him. And I assure you that I will pray for the success of this International Conference in Fatima".

Most. Rev. Hermann Raich, SVD
Bishop of Wabag, New Guinea

"With you I pray for the success of this conference and for all the means necessary to enable as many bishops as possible to attend".

Bishop William Kurtz
Kundiawa, New Guinea

"May God bless you all who are trying so hard to make Mary's request a reality".

Most Rev. Francis R. Lambert
Port Vila, Vanuatu (S.W. Pacific)

"Now that I know about the Fatima Peace Conference, I think it is a very meaningful initiative. Please be assured that I shall pray for this conference. I still remember you when you visited us last time in Taipei, and I pray God to bless all the preparatory work for the forthcoming conference".

Bishop Mattew Kia
Our Lady of China Church, Taiwan

"I will be with the Conference in spirit and will pray for its success. I will appreciate some literature that may come out of this Conference".

Rt. Rev. Dominic K. Andoh
Bishop of Accra, Ghana, West Africa

"On behalf of His Excellency Msgr. Hilarion Capucci, I express to you his gratitude for your invitation and he hopes that he will have the great pleasure of meeting you as soon as possible. We will be near you with your prayers and feelings for the success of the Fatima Peace Conference".

Father Isidore Battika
Secretery to Bishop Hilarion Capucci
Grec-Melkite Patriarch, Jerusalem

"I thank the Lord and Our Lady of Fatima for your perseverance, courage and patience in promoting the consecration of Russia to Our Lady".

Protacio G. Gungon, D.D.
Bishop of Antipolo, Philippines

"Father Gruner, I am all for you and the movement.

Therefore I will be offering a Mass for your intention, especially for the success of the discussion of the Collegial Consecration of Russia ... as a condition for World Peace".

Msgr. Nicholas Man Thang
Auxiliary Bishop, Mandalay, Burma

"I would like to offer the Holy Sacrifice of the Mass for the spiritual success of the Conference."

Msgr. A.J. Didjookarjono Pr.
Bishop of Surabaya-Indonesia

"Some priests of this diocese of Lisbon and I agree to offer the Holy Mass for the spiritual success of this Conference".

Antonio dos Reis Rodrigues
Auxiliary Bishop of Lisbon

"All those participating will most surely back your initiative for a clearer collegial act of consecration of Russia to the Immaculate Heart of Mary".

Bishop Walter Michael Ebejar, OP
Uniao da Vitoria, PR, Brazil

"Praying for the success of an important event so near to the heart of our Blessed Mother, I want to send you my blessing and good wishes".

Archbishop Roman Arrieta Villalobos
President of CECOR, San Jose, Costa Rica
Conferencia Episcopal de Costa Rica (CECOR)

"You have my promise of prayers for the success of your Mission and you may add my name to your list of Bishops who desire the Consecration of Russia to the Blessed Virgin Mary".

Bishop Rafael de la Barra

Prelatura de Illapel, Chile

"I will be present spiritually, through my prayers, at the conference. Please let me know if there is some way I can show my solidarity with you at the time of the conference through a letter or by some other means. May God continue to bless your good work of promoting devotion to our Blessed Mother and Her important message to us at Fatima".

Hilary Chavez Joya
Bishop-Prelate of Nuevo Casas Grandes
Mexico

Letters of Appreciation and Gratitude from Catholic Bishops to Father Nicholas Gruner After 1992 Conference:

Dear Father Gruner,

I don't know how to thank you for all the troubles you have taken to enable me to pay a visit to Fatima and take part in the Peace Conference. I will certainly remember this visit with immense gratitude for a long time to come. I fully understand the troubles and trials you had to face in the past and which you will have to face in the future also. I am sure the Lord will help you and give you the graces you need to play the role of a prophet. I assure you of my special prayers for all the intentions.

Please convey my blessings and gratitude to all the people working with you, whom I had the opportunity to meet at Fatima. On my way back to India, I spent three full days in Rome and I had an opportunity to be received for a private audience, with the Most Holy Father. It was a very brief audience and therefore I did not discuss with him what I had seen and heard in Fatima. In one word I tell you how impressed I was by your simplicity, humility and spirit of suffering.

I hope this finds you in the best of health. With the expression of my greeting for you and assuring you every blessings, I remain,

Yours fraternally in Our Lord,
Anthony Cardinal Padiyara
Archbishop of Ernakulam, Kerala, India

Jan. 17, 1993

Greetings from Mahenge/Tanzania,

After a one-week stay and conference in Fatima, I feel obliged to say a word of thanks to you for having given us the chance to be in the Sanctuary in Fatima. For us that was a great experience of the Christian life of prayer. We really felt much enriched by that prayerful experience, and we are grateful for all who organized our trip and cared for us during our stay in Fatima.

We came back safely and started at parish and even at Diocesan level to spread the Fatima Message.

Once again sincere thanks for all and I wish a very Happy and blessed New Year under the care of Our Lady of Fatima.

Yours Sincerely in Christ,
Rt. Rev. Patrick Iteka
Bishop of Mehenge.

Nov. 1, 1992

Dear Father,

I am back again in Agra, India after the most wonderful experience of my life at Fatima. It was really inspiring to be party of the rosary procession and concelebrated Masses on 12th and 13th October. Such deep faith, such devotion and such overflowing love for Our Blessed Mother of Fatima. Those were days of prayer and contemplation. I have no words to express my thanks to you and your helpers who made this possible and took such affectionate care of us. My prayers continue for you all.

The message of prayer, penance, rosary and charity was confirmed at Fatima. In my diocese of Agra that's the message I give to my people.

I cannot forget the unfortunate incidents that took place at the hallowed shrine of Fatima, and pray for love and forgiveness. God makes His sun to shine and rain to fall on everyone and we must learn to see His face in all His creation.

I would very much want to get the formula of consecration to the Immaculate Heart of Mary. When it is possible please send me a copy.

With good wishes and prayers for your work.

Yours Sincerely in Christ,

Most Rev. Cecil Desa

Bishop of Agra, India

April 17, 1993

Dear Friends,

I had not acknowledged in writing the kind help so that I could join the conference in Fatima last October but the bishop beneficiaries had already expressed their deep gratitude to Father Gruner verbally and publicly at the said meeting in Fatima. We expressed then publicly that without the material financial help of Catholics of Canada and America through Father Gruner and his generous collaborators the bishops would not be at Fatima. I do believe Our Lady willed it so. To Her and to you personally I express my sincere thank you.

I am one of those who admire the zeal and dedication of Father Gruner to the service of Our Lady. I pray She helps Father Gruner in the pursuit of his apostolate.

Let us pray for one another.

Thank you.

(Ret.) Archbishop Federico Limon, SVD

The Philippines

Dear Reverend Father,

You permitted me to live a Marian pilgrimage experience that has touched me deeply. As far as I am concerned, I prefer the climate of Fatima to the one of Lourdes. It's much easier to pray and meditate. As members of my diocese have a great devotion towards Mary, we will try to organize a beautiful site that we already have chosen for many years, to install there a large statue of Our Lady of Fatima. I will have to find that statue of Our Lady of Fatima.

Once more, thank you for enabling me to go to Fatima and I pray for you.

Please believe, Reverend Father, all my best fraternal wishes of respect.

Monseigneur Jean-Baptiste Some
The Bishop of Die Bougou, Burkina Faso

Dear Father Gruner,

I wish to express my deep appreciation and gratitude to you and your organization for inviting me to the Fatima Peace Conference and for sponsoring the trip. I am a child of Mary and the name Fatima was enough for me to jump at the invitation.

I was glad to be part of that Conference and to have listened to the message of Fatima explained in all its richness. I was one of those who spoke very little and maybe you can still recall what I said. I said that I believed that God and Our Lady had a purpose for bringing the Conference about and that you and ourselves the bishops, should listen and be attentive to one another and to what the Holy Spirit and Our Lady wanted to tell us.

I came home spiritually enriched and refreshed and thank God and the Fatima Crusaders for the opportunity.

Every best wish for Christmas to you and your team.

Rt. Reverend Dr. J.B. Adelakum
Bishop of Oyo Diocese, Nigeria

Dear Reverend Father Nicholas Gruner,

After my travel and my participation in the Conference of Peace in Fatima and also after the pleasant peregrination to Fatima, Tuy, Pontevedra and Compostela, I wish to thank you, my dear Father Gruner, for the opportunity which you had granted me. You are very kind and generous. All the Bishops have commented on your gentility and have eulogized your edifying piety for the Virgin Mother of Fatima. I can myself tell that the days of our pilgrimage together are profitable for my spiritual progress.

Thank you very much!
Cordially in Jesus and Mary,
D. Antonio de Mirnada
Bishop of Taubate, Brazil

Dear Father Leonard,

May I begin by thanking you for the letter you wrote to me on the First Saturday and for the copy of Father Paul Trinchard's book, *The Awesome Fatima Consecrations* you enclosed with it. Unfortunately the book was stolen on transit (evidently in some post office) but your letter and Archbishop Arulappa's arrived safely.

I was not able to go to Portugal for the Fatima meeting of Bishops, but I sent a representative. I hope it was successful.

I am most grateful to you, Father Gruner and to the many clients of Mary who, inspired by the love of the devotion to the Blessed Mother, are doing all you can to awaken the world to the stark reality of the Message of Fatima. As can be expected, many people, including bishops, are not only not interested but are even antagonistic. Nevertheless, in spite of their present negative attitude, the Marian movement is gathering momentum and I feel sure that Her Immaculate Heart will triumph in the end.

May I mention here that I belong to the first generation of Catholics in this part of Nigeria and happen to be the first native Nigerian to be made a Residential Bishop. After serving as Bishop of Umuahia for 30 years I am at present a retired Bishop and the Parochus of a small Parish (St. Theresa's). We are very grateful to God that the Church has made tremendous progress in Nigeria. But it is facing a serious Moslem threat that reminds one of that which Christianity in Africa suffered from the 5th to the 15th centuries.

From the look of things the only hope we have for the survival and growth in Nigeria and Africa, is in God through Our Lady of the Rosary. That is why, while praying for the salvation of the sinful world through the Rosary and the Immaculate Heart of Mary, we in Africa include our own peculiar petition for the liberation of the Church from the thralls of Mohammedanism and reconversion of Africa.

Assuring you of my prayers and begging for yours.
I remain,
Yours Gratefully in Jesus and Mary,
Anthony G. Nwedo, C.S.Sp.,
Bishop Emeritus of Umuabia, Nigeria

Appendix III

Sister Lucy Betrayed

By Christopher A. Ferrara

Introductory Note:*

In the 5th Century St. Jerome was confronted with a crude tract written by an obscure, unlettered young man named Helvidius, who denied the perpetual virginity of the Blessed Virgin Mary. Although St. Jerome ultimately responded to Helvidius, demolishing his flimsy arguments, the great saint had hesitated at first, "for fear that by replying I should be admitting that he posed a danger demanding confutation."

The same sort of problem arises in addressing two crude pamphlets produced in 1992 - 1993 by one Carlos Evaristo, an obscure young man from Portugal who claims to have interviewed Sister Lucy on two different occasions in her cloistered convent. According to Evaristo, during these two "interviews" Sister Lucy essentially retracted everything she had said about the Message of Fatima during the previous 75 years.

For nearly five years the pamphlets were justly ignored by the Catholic and secular press, having been immediately exposed as bunk by leading Fatima experts, including renowned French "Fatimist" Frère François de Marie des Anges. In 1998, however, the pamphlets resurfaced and received considerable publicity.

---

* By the editor of *The Fatima Crusader*.

This development prompted T*he Fatima Crusader* to commission the following article on Mr. Evaristo's notorious pamphlets. Although we, like St. Jerome, had some concern that by replying to Mr. Evaristo we "should be admitting that he posed a danger demanding confutation", the recent publicity for his pamphlets requires that we address the blatant contradictions of the Fatima Message that Evaristo has presented as the words of Sister Lucy.

Has Sister Lucy repudiated all of her prior statements about the consecration and conversion of Russia and the Third Secret of Fatima? Or is Mr. Evaristo the bearer of a "new" Message of Fatima, conveniently revised to meet the demands of "ecumania" and the New World Order taking shape around us? Read the evidence and the arguments marshaled by Mr. Ferrara and decide for yourself.

Introduction

This article presents a detailed discussion and analysis of two purported "interviews" with Sister Lucia de Jesus (known to Catholics as Sister Lucy), the last surviving seer of the apparitions of Our Lady of Fatima, who now lives as a cloistered nun in the Carmelite convent at Coimbra, Portugal. The purported interviews were allegedly conducted at the convent on October 11, 1992 and October 11, 1993 by one Carlos Evaristo, a self-styled "journalist, historian and interpreter."

Evaristo has published the interviews in the form of two pamphlets, entitled *Two Hours with Sister Lucy* and *It All Started with Two Hours with Sister Lucy.* The pamphlets have ignited tremendous controversy because in them Sister Lucy is reported as having flatly contradicted a whole series of statements she had made over the previous 75 years regarding the Message of Fatima and its implications for the Church and the world.

Before discussing the purported interviews in detail, it would be best to summarize the circumstances which surrounded their production and publication.

The Original Pamphlet

On October 11, 1992, Carlos Evaristo emerged from the famous convent in Coimbra, Portugal, to make an amazing claim: that he had just spent two hours interviewing Sister Lucy, and that during this "interview" she had contradicted all of her public and private statements over the past *75 years* concerning the Consecration of Russia to the Immaculate Heart of Mary, the conversion of Russia, and the Third Secret of Fatima.

According to Evaristo, the "new" Sister Lucy, contrary to everything she had said in some 75 years worth of prior correspondence, conversations and published remarks, was *now* saying that Russia had been consecrated to the Immaculate Heart of Mary (in 1984), that Russia is "converting", that "conversion" does not mean embracing the Catholic faith, and that the Third Secret of Fatima was not meant to be revealed to the faithful in 1960.

Evaristo would soon publish this first "interview" in the form of a crudely produced pamphlet entitled *Two Hours with Sister Lucy*. The credibility of the pamphlet was immediately cast into doubt by a manifestly absurd "detail" with which Evaristo embellished his account:

> "Carlos Evaristo, who was sitting closest to Sister Lucy and directly in front, *held Sister Lucy's hands for most of the two hour interview*."[1]

Sister Lucy is a cloistered nun who is not even permitted to see her blood relatives alone. The claim that she held hands for two hours with a strange man she had never met before was laughable on its face and impossible to believe.

Equally impossible to believe was the "interview" as a whole. In fact, it was so unbelievable that the only other Portuguese-speaking witness to Evaristo's alleged encounter with "Sister Lucy", Father Francisco Pacheco (who is a lawyer as well as a priest), publicly disavowed the pamphlet in its entirety:

> "I was the official translator of this meeting, which lasted two hours. I categorically affirm that the booklet entitled *Two Hours with Sister Lucy* published by Carlos Evaristo **contains lies and half-truths and is not to be believed**. When I was first shown a copy in January 1993, I immediately contacted Carlos Evaristo and I personally told him **not to publish this booklet because of the gross lies that he had put in it** ... I trust that this will end the confusion caused by Carlos Evaristo and his **notorious pamphlet**."[2]

Besides Father Pacheco, two other witnesses were present during the alleged 1992 "interview", but neither of them speaks Portuguese. Anthony Cardinal Padiyara and Bishop Francis Michaelappa, both from India, were in Fatima to attend a Marian conference at the invitation of Father Nicholas Gruner's Fatima apostolate, and they went along with Evaristo and Father Pacheco to the convent at Coimbra. Afterwards, Cardinal Padiyara would only attest that he had been present during the "interview", which was conducted entirely in a language he did not understand. As for Bishop Michaelappa, he not only refused to vouch for the authenticity of the "interview", but joined Father Pacheco in demanding that Evaristo not publish it.

Why did Father Pacheco publicly repudiate *Two Hours with Sister Lucy*, and why did both he and Bishop Michaelappa demand that it not be published by Evaristo? The answer was supplied by Evaristo himself: In a fax transmission to Coralie Graham, editor of *The Fatima Crusader*, Evaristo admitted that the statements he had attributed to "Sister Lucy" contain:

> "... contradictory and unlogical (*sic*) things which at times seem almost *craziness*."[3]

In the same fax Evaristo further admits: "The dialogue was not recorded at the time. *No notes were taken*."[4] As if to demolish any remaining vestige of credibility in the "interview", Evaristo even concedes that because his memory is unreliable, the "transcript" of the "interview" did not reflect his own memory but was "reconstructed"(!) from the memory of others:

> "Although I may have a *bad memory* this *reconstruction* of what was said was not largely made by me. *I only typed it*."[5]

This is a devastating admission, because if the "transcript" was not based on Evaristo's own memory of what "Sister Lucy" allegedly said, and if Father Pacheco, the only other Portuguese-speaking witness, repudiated the "transcript" because it "contains lies and half-truths and is not to be believed", then the only possible sources for the "transcript" are Cardinal Padiyara and Bishop Michaelappa — *neither of whom speaks a word of Portuguese*.

Yet, nowhere in *Two Hours with Sister Lucy* is the public ever told that the "transcript" of the "interview" with Sister Lucy is not really a transcript at all, but a "reconstruction" from the memories of people who could not even speak the interviewee's language!

Evaristo Tries Again

Following massive public criticism of the ridiculous statements attributed to "Sister Lucy" in *Two Hours with Sister Lucy,* Evaristo produced a second pamphlet, which he entitled *It All Started with Two Hours with Sister Lucy.* The sequel simply re-publishes the original fabricated "transcript", but this time attempts to buttress it with another purported "interview" which allegedly took place on October 11, 1993 — a year to the day after the first interview. In this second interview the remarks attributed to Sister Lucy are briefer and vaguer than those in the first "interview", and she does not repeat her remarks about the Third Secret of Fatima not being meant for the faithful.

In contrast with the original pamphlet, which was justly ignored by the press, the 1993 sequel received considerable publicity in 1998, including coverage on a Spanish television show and articles in the periodicals *Christus* (of Portugal) and *Gente* (of Italy). That the sequel has acquired such publicity makes a refutation of its glaring incredibility a matter of considerable urgency.

Evaristo claims that the second interview was audio and video-taped in the presence of himself and eight other witnesses who allegedly attended, including a Cardinal. The alleged audio and video tapes have not, however, been made available to the public.

Evaristo further claims that this second interview was conducted on *one hour's notice* to the Mother Prioress of the Convent, after the Cardinal (His Eminence Ricardo Cardinal Vidal of Cebu, Philippines) spontaneously decided that a group of nine people, including Evaristo, should jump into cars and pay Sister Lucy a visit late at night with a video camera and a tape recorder! We are told that this hastily assembled crowd and its equipment was admitted into a cloistered convent at *10:30 p.m.* to interview an 86-year-old nun who would normally be asleep at that hour.

As with the first interview, the reader is asked to believe that "Sister Lucy" now contradicts everything she had said publicly and privately about the Message of Fatima for more than 75 years before she spoke to Mr. Evaristo and his witnesses.

Oddly enough, although a Cardinal and 7 other witnesses were supposedly in attendance at the 1993 spontaneous late-night interview of "Sister Lucy", Evaristo's sequel does not contain any attestations by these alleged witnesses that the "transcript" of the 1993 interview accurately reflects what "Sister Lucy" supposedly said on that occasion.

The purpose of this article is not to draw any final conclusions about which theory best explains the incredible "retractions" contained in these two "interviews" of "Sister Lucy". It is not necessary for our purposes to determine whether "Sister Lucy's" repudiation of her own statements is attributable to treachery on the part of Evaristo, or whether the woman in nun's garb he allegedly interviewed at the convent in Coimbra was an imposter (as some have theorized), or whether it was indeed Sister Lucy who said the things attributed to her, but only as the result of duress, obedience to the suggestions of her superiors, or the effects of declining mental acuity combined with the suasion of others.

No matter which scenario is chosen, the conclusion is the same: Sister Lucy has been betrayed by those who are promoting her "retractions".

This article does not seek to establish as fact a particular scenario for this betrayal, but only to demonstrate that a betrayal must have occurred because the statements attributed to Sister Lucia de Jesus in both the 1992 and the 1993 "interviews" are plainly unworthy of belief, for these reasons:

First of all, they contradict the Message of Fatima itself, which, as Cardinal Ratzinger has noted, "three Popes have already recognized in the most solemn manner possible and have whole-heartedly taken part in this devotion";[6]

Second, they contradict Sister Lucy's own repeated prior statements about the Message and its meaning over a period of seventy-five years before the Evaristo "interviews";

Third, they contradict the evidence of our own senses regarding the drastic moral and spiritual deterioration of the world since the papal consecration of the world (but not Russia specifically) in 1984, and the supposed "fall of Communism" thereafter.

The First "Interview":
Two Hours with Sister Lucy

As we have seen, the most obvious problem with the pamphlet *Two Hours with Sister Lucy* is that it deceptively presents as a *verbatim* transcript what is nothing more than a "reconstruction" of what Sister Lucy allegedly said, a "reconstruction" which is not based on Evaristo's own memory but on the memory of "witnesses" who do not even speak Portuguese. *The original pamphlet never mentions this crucial fact,* but leads the reader to believe that "Sister Lucy" is being quoted word-for-word.

Only in the sequel pamphlet, *It All Started with Two Hours with Sister Lucy,* did Evaristo finally admit that what he had originally presented to the public as a verbatim transcript is a fictitious reconstruction:

This [the first interview] *is not a literal transla-tion*. It is a *conceptual* translation. The language used in this document is *based* on the actual Portuguese dialogue ...?[7]

What does Evaristo mean by a "conceptual" transla-tion? What does he mean when he says the translation is "based" on the "actual Portuguese dialogue"? And why did Evaristo fail to inform the public in the first place that his much-vaunted "interview" of "Sister Lucy," which had caused so much controversy and even out-rage around the world, contains only *concepts* and not her actual words?

That a "conceptual" reconstruction of a conver-sation was presented to the public as a *verbatim* transcript should be enough to discredit the first pamphlet entirely, along with any further products by its author. The republication of the admittedly fab-ricated "interview" in the sequel pamphlet does nothing to improve its credibility today, more than five years af-ter the alleged "interview" of "Sister Lucy" took place.

Putting aside, for the moment, the obvious problems with the credibility of the original "interview", the reader is now invited simply to consider, in themselves, the words which Evaristo ascribes to his 1992 version of "Sister Lucy."

On the Consecration of Russia

"Sister Lucy":

> Yes, yes, yes ... The consecration of Russia was already partially done. Pope Pius XII made it in 1942 on October 31, but it lacked union with all of the bishops of the world, which Pope John Paul fi-nally managed to unite in 1984.

Evaristo:

So this consecration [1984] was then accepted by Our Lady?

"Sister Lucy":

Yes![8]

How are we to reconcile what Evaristo now *admits* was a fabricated "transcript" with all of Sister Lucy's prior statements to the effect that neither the 1982 consecration nor the 1984 consecration fulfilled Our Lady's request?

For example, there is Sister Lucy's September 1985 interview in *Sol de Fatima*, the Blue Army's official publication in Spain:

Question:

John Paul II had invited all the bishops to join in the consecration of Russia, which he was going to make at Fatima on May 13, 1982, and which he was to renew at the end of the Holy Year in Rome on March 25, 1984, before the original statue of Our Lady of Fatima. Has he not therefore done what was requested at Tuy?

Sister Lucy:

There was *no participation of all the bishops* and there was *no mention of Russia*.

Question:

So the consecration was *not done* as requested by Our Lady?

Sister Lucy:

No. Many bishops attached no importance to this act.

Sister Lucy's statements in the *Sol de Fatima* interview are completely consistent with all of her other prior statements about the requirements for a valid consecration of Russia to the Immaculate Heart of Mary: (a) that it be done solemnly and publicly by the Pope, (b) in union with all the world's bishops, and (c) with *specific mention* of Russia.

This is precisely what Sister Lucy told the Papal Nuncio to Portugal, Most Rev. Sante Portalupi, when he met with her on March 21, 1982, to discuss how the Consecration which the Pope had planned for May 13 of that year should be carried out:

> "Sister Lucy explained that the Pope must choose a date upon which His Holiness commands the bishops of the entire world to make, each in his own Cathedral and at the same time as the Pope, a solemn and public ceremony of Reparation and Consecration of *Russia* ..."[9]

As if that were not enough, on May 12, 1982, the day before the attempted 1982 consecration, *L'Osservatore Romano* (Italian edition) published a 1978 interview of Sister Lucy by Father Umberto Maria Pasquale, a Salesian priest, who was "the confidant of the seer of Fatima since 1939".[10] During her interview of August 5, 1978, she told Father Umberto in no uncertain terms that Our Lady had *not* requested the consecration of the world in general, but of *Russia specifically, and only Russia*:

> At a certain moment I said to her: "Sister, I should like to ask you a question. If you cannot answer me, let it be. But if you can answer it, I would be most grateful to you ... Has Our Lady ever spoken to you about the consecration of *the world* to Her Immaculate Heart?" "*No*, Father Umberto! *Never*! At the Cova da Iria in 1917 Our Lady had promised: *I shall come to ask for the consecration of Russia* ... In 1929, at Tuy, as She had promised,

Our Lady came back to tell me that the moment had come to ask the Holy Father for the consecration of *that country* (Russia)."[11]

After this conversation, Father Umberto asked Sister Lucy to put this clarification in writing. Her handwritten note was first published in a 1980 pamphlet produced by Cavaleiro da Imaculado, establishing beyond any doubt that the consecration of "the world" *did not suffice* to fulfill Our Lady's request at Fatima, as Sister Lucy herself would later say after *both* the 1982 and 1984 consecration ceremonies. The following is a translation of the letter written by Sister Lucy to Father Umberto on April 13, 1980.

Reverend Father Umberto,

In replying to your question, I will clarify: Our Lady of Fatima, in Her request, referred *only to the consecration of Russia;* in the letter which I wrote to the Holy Father Pius XII — at the direction of my confessor — I asked for the consecration of the world with explicit mention of Russia. Yours devotedly and in union of prayers. Coimbra, April 13, 1980.

(Signed) Sister Lucy.

Here Sister Lucy confirms to the whole Church that the consecration of the world is *extraneous* to the Message of Fatima, and represents, at most, the suggestion of her confessor. This suggestion seems to have resulted from a command by the Bishop of Gurza that Sister Lucy address to Pius XII a request for the consecration of the world (in addition to Russia), in her letter of December 2, 1940.[12]

Precisely because the attempted consecration in 1982 made no mention of Russia (and the bishops did not participate), Sister Lucy told the Papal Nuncio on March 19, 1983 that:

"The Consecration of Russia *has not been done as Our Lady requested*. I was not able to make this statement before because I did not have the permission of the Holy See."[13]

Even Evaristo admits in his sequel pamphlet that the 1982 Consecration was insufficient because "there was no participation by the bishops, making it *invalid*."[14]

Indeed, how could the Pope consecrate Russia without even *mentioning* Russia? The notion offends simple logic and common sense. Yet the "Sister Lucy" who allegedly spoke to Carlos Evaristo in October 1992 offered this curious explanation, which contradicts everything she had said before:

Evaristo:

But does not Russia have to be specifically mentioned, and did not Our Lady say this?

"Sister Lucy":

The Pope's intention was Russia when he said "those peoples ..." in the text of the 1984 consecration ... God knew that the Pope's intention was Russia and he meant "Russia" in the consecration. What is important is his intention, *like when a priest has the intention to Consecrate a Host*.

But as "Sister Lucy" should be expected to know, the mere unspoken intention to Consecrate a Host does not suffice to bring about the transubstantiation of mere bread into the Body of Christ. That is precisely the point: The priest must *say aloud certain specific words* — "This is My Body" — in order to carry out Our Lord's command at the Last Supper. Absolutely no other words will do in their place.

In his original pamphlet Evaristo avoids mentioning a critical fact which demolishes any claim that the words "those peoples" are just as good as the crucial word "Russia": After Pope John Paul had said the words "those peoples" while reciting the 1984 Consecration in St. Peter's Square, he spontaneously added the following words to the prepared text:

> " ... of which You Yourself are *awaiting* our consecration and confiding."

While the added phrase does not appear in the prepared text printed before the 1984 Consecration of the world, it does appear in the report of what the Pope actually said in *L'Osservatore Romano*.[15] As the Pope's spontaneous addition to the text establishes, "those peoples" — the peoples of Russia — *were still awaiting* Consecration to the Immaculate Heart on March 25, 1984. Russia was *not* consecrated in St. Peter's Square on that date because, for whatever reason, the Pope had determined that a Consecration of Russia *by name* was not expedient.

This is confirmed beyond doubt by a report in *Avvenire*, the Italian Catholic Bishops' newspaper, which notes that several hours *after* His Holiness had recited the act of consecration, he again addressed Our Lady of Fatima, this time inside St. Peter's Basilica, stating in the presence of 10,000 witnesses:

> "We wished to choose this Sunday for the act of entrusting and consecration of the world ... of all peoples, especially those who have a very great need of this consecration and entrustment, of those peoples of whom You Yourself are *awaiting* our act of consecration."[16]

So, hours after His Holiness had recited the 1984 act of Consecration in St. Peter's Square, he clearly understood that Russia ("those peoples") was *still awaiting* consecration to Mary's Immaculate Heart, and that he had yet to perform the act. And, as we have shown in the quote above, in September 1985 Sister Lucy publicly stated in *Sol de Fatima* magazine that the 1984 consecration ceremony *did not fulfill Our Lady's request*.

In any case, it should be obvious that when God commands the public consecration of a particular thing, it means that this particular thing must be *mentioned* to the public. A public consecration of Russia which does not even *mention* Russia is, therefore, no public consecration at all, but a mere private, unspoken wish. One might as well claim that the Pope could publicly consecrate Russia to the Immaculate Heart of Mary by merely thinking to himself — "I consecrate Russia." — while strolling in the Vatican gardens! The very notion is ridiculous.

Yet it is precisely this ridiculous notion which is now adopted by the "new" Sister Lucy, who contradicts today everything she has said for the past seven decades about the specific requirements for the Consecration of Russia:

Evaristo:

But doesn't Our Lady want Russia to be *specifically* mentioned?

"Sister Lucy":

Our Lady never requested that Russia be specifically mentioned by name (!). At the time I didn't even know what Russia was. We [all three Fatima seers] thought she was a very wicked woman. (!)

Are we now to believe, after all these years, that when Our Lady came to Fatima to request the Consecration of Russia to Her Immaculate Heart, She did not care whether Russia was even *mentioned*? Does it seem likely that the Queen of Heaven would neglect to make it clear to the seers of Fatima that Russia is a *nation*, not some "wicked woman"?

We know that this cannot be true simply on the basis of Sister Lucy's statement to Father Fuentes, the Vice Postulator of the cause of Jacinta and Francisco, on December 26, 1957:

> "Father, the Most Holy Virgin is very sad because no one has paid any attention to Her message, *neither the good nor the bad*. The good continue on their way, but without giving any importance to Her Message. Tell them, Father, that many times the Most Holy Virgin told my cousins Francisco and Jacinta, as well as myself, that many nations will disappear from the face of the earth. She said that ***Russia** will be the instrument of chastisement chosen by Heaven to punish the whole world if we do not beforehand obtain the conversion of that poor **nation**...*"[17]

This statement alone establishes beyond all dispute that the seers of Fatima understood from the beginning that the very essence of the Message of Fatima requires the conversion of the *nation* of Russia as a sign of God's grace at work in our times.

What is more, in the course of *four* detailed memoirs about the apparitions at Fatima, Sister Lucy had never indicated the slightest confusion about the meaning of the word "Russia". Nor can we find *anything* Sister Lucy wrote or said to anyone in the world before Evaristo's 1992 "interview" which would suggest that the Fatima seers did not understand, from the very beginning, that Russia is a nation singled out by God for a special act of consecration that would bring about the conversion of that nation and peace in the world.

But the new "Sister Lucy" now claims that the Fatima seers were all ignorant of the most basic meaning of what Our Lady told them, and that Heaven itself did nothing to disabuse them of their ignorance! This, of course, is completely impossible. Therefore, something is seriously amiss at the convent in Coimbra.

In any case, it is absurd that an act as important as the Consecration of Russia to the Immaculate Heart of Mary — an act specifically commanded by Our Lord Himself through His Blessed Mother — should now become the subject of a worldwide guessing game, in which the faithful are left to argue about the meaning of the vague phrase "those peoples". Is *this* how the Church of God carries out the command of God? With an equivocation? We are certainly permitted to ask ourselves, and each other, why in Heaven's name was Russia *not* mentioned specifically in 1984 so as to end all doubt about the matter? What possible impediment could there have been to the simple utterance of one word — "Russia"?

It is no wonder that Evaristo himself admitted that there are "contradictory and unlogical things which seem almost craziness" in these "two hours with Sister Lucy" — two hours which he himself concedes (however belatedly) were "reconstructed" from the "memory" of witnesses who do not even speak Sister Lucy's language!

On the Conversion of Russia

Now, if Catholics believe anything, they believe that their Church is the sole ark of salvation and that (invincible ignorance aside) *conversion* to the one true religion is objectively necessary for the salvation of souls. As Our Lord Himself warned us just before He ascended into Heaven:

> "He that believeth and is baptized shall be saved: but he that believeth not shall be condemned." [Mark 16:16]

When Our Lady came to Fatima She brought with Her a divine warning and a divine promise, with the promise being contingent upon *conversion* to the one true religion:

> "You have seen hell, where the souls of poor sinners go. To *save them,* God wishes to establish in the world *devotion to My Immaculate Heart* ... If what I say to you is done, many *souls will be saved*, and there will be peace ... In the end, My Immaculate Heart will triumph. The Holy Father will consecrate *Russia* to Me, which *will be converted*".

In the context of the Message of Fatima, conversion can obviously mean only one thing: embrace of the Catholic Faith. The Catholic Church has defined three times *ex cathedra* that outside the Church there is no salvation:

Ex cathedra: There is but one universal Church of the faithful, outside of which no one at all is saved. (Pope Innocent III, the Fourth Lateran Council, 1215)

Ex cathedra: We declare, say, define, and pronounce that it is absolutely necessary for the salvation of every human creature to be subject to the Roman Pontiff. (Pope Boniface VIII, the Bull *Unam Sanctam*, 1302)

Ex cathedra: The most Holy Roman Catholic Church firmly believes, professes, and preaches that none of those existing outside the Catholic Church, not only pagans, but also Jews and heretics and schismatics, can have a share in life eternal; but that they will go into the eternal fire which was prepared for the devil and his angels, unless before death they are joined with Her; and that so important is the unity of this ecclesiastical body that only those remaining within this unity can receive an eternal recompense for their fasts, their almsgivings, their other works of Christian piety and the duties of a Christian soldier. *No one,* let his almsgiving be as great as it may, *no one*, even if he pour out his blood for the name of Christ, can be saved, unless he remain within the bosom and the unity of the Catholic Church. (Pope Eugene IV, the Bull *Cantate Domino,* 1441).

In view of these pronouncements, anyone who says there is salvation outside the Catholic Church is denying the Catholic Faith. In one way or another, all of the souls in Heaven enter as members of the Catholic Church.[18]

Therefore, when Our Lady said that Russia will be converted, She can only have meant a conversion to Catholicism. Nothing less than becoming Catholic could constitute a true conversion, because the Catholic religion is the religion established by God Himself.

God did not establish the Russian Orthodox Church, whose doctrines differ very significantly from the doctrine of the religion God established. For example, the Russian Orthodox Church rejects: the Papal primacy; the teaching of the Catholic Church on divorce and remarriage; the Catholic teaching that the Holy Spirit proceeds from the Father and the Son together, not simply from the Father; Catholic doctrine on Purgatory; and the Catholic dogma of the Immaculate Conception of Mary.

On this last point of doctrine, God has decreed that souls are to be *saved* by devotion to the Immaculate Heart of Mary. Obviously those souls must first *believe* in the Immaculate Heart of Mary as an object of faith — that is, they must be Catholic, since the doctrine of the Immaculate Conception of Mary is *unique to the Cath-*

olic Church, which is the one true Church of God.

Further, if "in the end, My Immaculate Heart will triumph", as Our Lady prophesied at Fatima, then Our Lady must be recognized by the *nations* of the world for what She is — and first of all by Russia. Hence the conversion of Russia can only mean that Russia will become a Catholic nation, because the Russian Orthodox religion does not admit as a doctrine that Mary was immaculately conceived and free from all sin whatsoever during Her earthly life.

Therefore, *without a conversion of Russia to the Catholic Faith, the Message of Fatima is completely and utterly meaningless.*

Indeed, if Russian Orthodoxy were acceptable to God, why would He have sent His Mother to Fatima in 1917 to speak of the conversion of Russia, when it was already Orthodox?

But what does this strange new "Sister Lucy" who appears on the pages of Evaristo's admittedly fabricated "transcript" have to say on the all-important subject of the *conversion* of Russia through devotion to the Immaculate Heart? It defies belief:

Evaristo:

      Has the conversion of Russia then taken place?

"Sister Lucy":

      Yes. The news speaks for themselves (*sic*).

Yes, the "news" does speak for itself; but the news does not tell us that Russia is converting. On the contrary, the "news" tells us that Russia has just enacted a new law which discriminates *against* the Catholic Church and in favor of Russian Orthodoxy, Judaism, Buddhism and Islam. This new law requires that the few Catholic parishes which exist in Russia apply for annual registration, along with other "foreign sects" —

registration which can be revoked at will by any local Russian bureaucrat in any town in Russia. *The same law forbids Holy Mother Church to "proselytize" among non-Catholics in Russia.* In other words, Russia has just made it illegal for the Catholic Church to seek the conversion of Russia! Yet the new "Sister Lucy" tells us that Russia is "converting"!

There is more "news" which Evaristo's "Sister Lucy" seems to have missed: Classroom "sex education" has just been introduced into Russia over the protests of *non-Catholic psychologists*, while Poland — the Pope's own country — has embraced both classroom sex-education *and* "legalized" abortion since the "consecration" of Russia in 1984.

Meanwhile, in the world at large some 600 million innocent children have been slaughtered in the womb since the "conversion of Russia" in 1984. What sort of "conversion" results in the death of 600 million children in the womb? Only a conversion to satan. And that is precisely what we have seen in Russia and the world at large since the "consecration" of 1984.

There are a few other important items missing from the "news" filtering into the convent which houses the new "Sister Lucy": The news that euthanasia is being legalized around the world, and that human cloning will soon follow. The news that all the nations of the world are moving toward a "New World Order" in which contraception, abortion on demand, divorce and homosexual relations are viewed as "rights", while the Church's moral teaching is defied by politicians and mocked by the mass media. The new "Sister Lucy" also seems ignorant of the news that wars and persecutions of Catholics around the world, especially in Russia and China, have *increased* since 1984.

Considering the following item in Evaristo's 1992 "conceptual" interview with "Sister Lucy", we might wonder whether it is "news" or pure fantasy which "Sister Lucy" is receiving in the convent at Coimbra:

"Sister Lucy":

> [T]hat man in Russia, unknowingly was an instrument of God in the conversion ...

Evaristo:

> What man? Gorbachev?

"Sister Lucy":

> Yes, and when he visited the Holy Father in Rome, he knelt at his feet and asked pardon for all the crimes he had committed in his life.

There is one small problem with this bit of "news". *The Vatican denies that it ever happened.* Commenting on a Spanish television report about this alleged revelation by Sister Lucy, the Pope's spokesman, Joaquin Navarro-Valls, declared as follows:

> "Gorbachev did not ask for forgiveness from the Pope ... Mikhail Gorbachev did not kneel before the Pope and beg forgiveness for his sins, as supposedly stated by Sister Lucy ... It is neither true *nor plausible* ..."[19]

Here the maxim "false in one, false in all" would seem to apply. If it can be shown that the new "Sister Lucy" has uttered at least one thing which "is neither true nor plausible", as the Vatican itself declares, then Evaristo's entire "interview" of this strange new "Sister Lucy" should, in prudence, be rejected. All the more so, in view of Evaristo's admitted technique of presenting fabricated "conceptual" translations as *verbatim* transcripts.

In any case, the truth of the matter is that after his meeting with the Pope at the Vatican, during which he repented of absolutely nothing, Mr. Gorbachev returned to his chairmanship of the globalist Gorbachev Foundation, which busily promotes reduction of the world's population by several **billion** people through a strict regime of contraception and abortion. Of such horrors is the "conversion of Russia" made, according to the new "Sister Lucy".

The New Meaning of Conversion

As we can see, the new "Sister Lucy" has an entirely new idea about what "conversion" really means. It goes along with her entirely new idea about what the "consecration of Russia" really means. Here is what the new "Sister Lucy" has to say about the new meaning of conversion:

Evaristo:

> But is the conversion of Russia not interpreted as the conversion of the Russian people to Catholicism?

"Sister Lucy":

> *Our Lady never said that.* There are many misinterpretations around. The fact is that Russia, the communist, atheist power, prevented the people from carrying out their faith. *People now have an individual choice to remain as they are or convert.* This they are now free to do, and many conversions are in fact taking place ...

Our Lady never said that? Here the new "Sister Lucy" drives a dagger through the heart of our Faith. She tells us that Our Lady did not come to earth at Fatima to seek souls for the Church of which She is the Mother, but rather "an individual choice to remain as they are or convert"!

So, the miracle to be produced by the consecration of Russia and the triumph of the Immaculate Heart of Mary is not the salvation of many millions of souls through reception of the precious gift of the Catholic faith, but only "individual choice"! No serious Catholic could be expected to believe this pluralistic drivel attributed to Sister Lucy, who actually saw the Mother of God six times at Fatima, and who was horrified to see the many souls burning in hell for all eternity because of their "individual choice."

Has the new "Sister Lucy" not considered that long before the 1984 "consecration" the entire Western world had "individual choice"? "The individual choice" to kill babies in the womb; "the individual choice" to contracept; the "individual choice" to divorce; the "individual choice" to indulge in pornography or homosexual relations; and even "the individual choice" to become a Catholic, if one happened to be among the few so inclined in our increasingly amoral civilization. Does this mean that the West had "converted" before Russia did, according to "Sister Lucy's" new definition of the word? Does the triumph of the Immaculate Heart of Mary mean nothing more, in the end, than the spread of *pluralistic democracy* to another country?

We cannot fail to note that even this worldly "miracle" of "individual choice" has yet to occur in Russia. On the contrary, as we have seen, Russia has just enacted a law forbidding the Catholic Church to seek converts among the Russian people and limiting the freedom of the Church even to exist in "that poor nation". So Russia is not even a liberal democracy, let alone a Catholic country today. Yet the new "Sister Lucy" now tells us that Russia is converting.

And where are these "many conversions" which the new "Sister Lucy" says are now taking place all over Russia? Like the fabled repentance of Gorbachev on his knees before the Pope, they are pure fantasy. In all of Russia today there are only 300,000 Catholics. *Catholics in Russia are outnumbered by Muslims ten-to-one.* In fact, there are far more converts to Islam than to Catholicism. Even worse, there were at least 300,000-500,000 Catholics in Russia at the time of the Russian Revolution — significantly more than today — and today there are fewer Catholic parishes in Russia than there were in 1917! Thus, the Church has been *losing ground* in Russia since it began "converting" in 1984.[20]

Still worse, since the 1984 "consecration of Russia" proselytization by Catholics has not only been forbidden by the law of Russia, but *by the Vatican itself:* In 1993 at Balamand, Lebanon, Vatican officials negotiated a joint statement with the Russian Orthodox Church. The Balamand Statement declares that in Russia "there is *no question of conversion of people from one Church to the other* in order to insure their salvation"; that the return of the Russian Orthodox to the Catholic Church is an "outdated ecclesiology", and that the Catholic Church will exclude "for the future *all proselytization* and all desire by Catholics for expansion at the expense of the Orthodox Church."[21] At Fatima, Our Lady spoke of the conversion of Russia; but at Balamand, Vatican officials agreed that *the conversion of Russia is no longer necessary.* Yet the new "Sister Lucy" now tells us that Russia has been "converting" for the past sixteen years!

Compare this abysmal situation with the *true* miracle which occurred in Mexico after the apparition of Our Lady of Guadalupe in 1531: some seven million

Mexicans — virtually the entire nation — converted to the Catholic faith within nine years. And in Portugal itself the apparitions of Our Lady at Fatima worked a similar miracle, causing the Masonic-Socialist government of that nation to topple and the Reign of Christ the King to be reestablished in that nation within nine years of the Miracle of the Sun at Cova da Iria.

But those were the days when conversion meant conversion. Today, in the mind of the new "Sister Lucy", in the mind of the world at large, many words have lost their meaning — even the words of Heaven at Fatima. In the Church today we see that the poison of Modernism, condemned by Pope St. Pius X as "the synthesis of all heresies", has seeped into the thinking of many, even prelates. And now it corrupts the once-pure testimony of Sister Lucy of Fatima. In true Modernist fashion this new "Sister Lucy" uses all the traditional words — consecration, conversion, peace — but invests them with false new meanings which completely contradict their true meanings.

In Evaristo's new "Sister Lucy" we see also a perfect example of the Modernist confusion between faith and politics in the post-conciliar Church, where Vatican diplomacy and *Ostpolitik* seem to have taken precedence over the propagation of the Catholic Faith for the salvation of souls from hell, a place which is not even mentioned any longer. This confusion between faith and politics, between the supernatural and the natural orders is what leads the new "Sister Lucy" of the Carlos Evaristo pamphlets to declare that the granting of a mere appearance of "individual choice" by a still-godless civil government is a supernatural miracle of "conversion".

What sort of "Sister Lucy" is it, then, who could look upon the awful developments in Russia and the world since 1984 and see in them the *fulfillment* of the promises of Our Lady of Fatima? It is a Sister Lucy we have never known; a Modernist Sister Lucy whose strange new words make a mockery of everything she said before. It is a New Fatima for the New Church which the Modernists say was created at the Second Vatican Council.

There is neither conversion nor triumph in this new Message of Fatima; there is only a pathetic accommodation to the worldly wisdom of a dying world: "People now have an individual choice to remain as they are *or* convert." A conversion of Russia without conversion to the Catholic Faith. What an insult to Our Lady of Fatima. And what an infinite insult to Him who sent Her.

On the Third Secret of Fatima

When Sister Lucy placed the Third Secret of Fatima into a sealed envelope in 1944 and sent it to the Bishop of Leiria-Fatima, she made him promise that it would definitely be opened and *read to the world* either at her death or in 1960, whichever would come first. So testified Canon Galamba, the personal friend to the first Bishop of Fatima, Bishop da Silva, whose testimony is contained in the files of Father Alonso, the official Fatima archivist appointed by the Ordinary of the Diocese of Leiria-Fatima.

On September 7, 1946, Cardinal Cerejeira, the Patriarch of Portugal, publicly confirmed at a Marian Congress that the Third Secret has been written and placed in a sealed envelope and *"will be opened* in 1960." In conversations with Sister Lucy in October 1946, Canon Barthas asked her "When will the Third Secret be *revealed to us*?", and she replied: "In 1960." When Canon Barthas asked her why 1960 and not sooner, she replied: "Because the Blessed Virgin wishes it so." Sister Lucy told no less than Cardinal Ottaviani that 1960 was the year chosen by Our Lady because in that year the Secret "will seem clearer" (*mais claro*).

In 1960 the whole Catholic world awaited disclosure of the Third Secret. There was even an American television show entitled "Zero 1960", whose theme was the expected disclosure of the Secret. But, as we know, it was not to be. In February 1960 the Vatican, which had received the text of the Secret in 1957, announced through a Portuguese press agency that the Secret had been suppressed by Pope John and would probably "remain forever under absolute seal."

As the post-conciliar debacle unfolded over the next 35 years, a growing number of Catholics became convinced that the Third Secret must have predicted what would happen after the Council, and that this is why Sister Lucy had said the Secret "will be clearer" by 1960. By 1960 the Second Vatican Council had been announced.

How sad it is to see that in 1992, at the convent in Coimbra, the "Sister Lucy" of the Carlos Evaristo pamphlet would turn her back on this aspect, too, of the Message of Fatima.

Evaristo:

> But didn't Our Lady say that it [the Third Secret] was to be revealed to the public by 1960, at the latest?

"Sister Lucy":

> Our Lady never said that. Our Lady said it was for the Pope.

For the *Pope*? Then what of Sister Lucy's statements to Canon Galamba, Canon Barthas, the Patriarch of Portugal and Cardinal Ottaviani, all to the effect that the Third Secret of Fatima, like the first two Secrets, was for the *whole world*? What of the very envelope in which Sister Lucy herself had placed the Secret, and which was photographed for *Life* magazine [1/3/49]; the envelope on which Bishop da Silva had written: "This envelope with its contents shall be entrusted to His Eminence Cardinal Manuel (Cerejeira), Patriarch of Lisbon, after my death" — the very Cardinal who publicly confirmed that the Secret would be opened and read to the world in 1960! What of the Vatican's *refusal* in 1944 to accept delivery of the text of the Secret supposedly meant for the Pope? What of Cardinal Cerejeira's declaration in 1960, when Pope John ultimately suppressed the Secret, contrary to all expectations: "I affirm categorically that I was not consulted." And, finally, what of the Vatican's own 1960 press release, which announces the suppression of the Secret, but does *not* give as a reason that the Secret was "meant for the Pope."

Throughout all these events, and for decades thereafter, Sister Lucy had never even suggested that the Third Secret of Fatima was meant only for the Pope. No, it was meant for us, and the whole Catholic world knew it. Indeed, before the Blue Army became the instrument of Fatima revisionism (along with the new "Sister Lucy"), its leader, John Haffert, expressed the disillusionment of Catholics everywhere over the unexpected suppression of the Secret:

> "1960 came and went and the Pope 'to whom the Secret had been confided' did not make it public ... The silence from Rome lay heavily on all of us. People began to murmur that Fatima must have been a fake, that there was no Secret, that the 1960 Secret was 'a hoax'... [in 1964], the effect of the

215

long silence concerning the 1960 Secret still seemed to hang over us like a pall."[22]

At the convent in Coimbra in 1992 the "Sister Lucy" presented to the world by Carlos Evaristo completely rewrote the Message of Fatima. We have seen that even Evaristo was forced to admit privately that this new "Sister Lucy" had uttered "contradictory and unlogical things which at times seem almost craziness", that his memory was bad, and that the whole "interview" was a "reconstruction" based on the memory of others who did not even speak Portuguese.

But in 1993 Evaristo would tell the world, in his great sequel, that the illogical and crazy things he had "reconstructed" the year before were the purest truth.

The Second "Interview" Less of the Same

As our discussion of the 1992 "interview" should make clear, its publication proved to be a severe embarrassment to Evaristo. Hence his second attempt in 1993 to corroborate the capitulation of the last surviving seer of Fatima.

But here we have not more of the same, but *less* of the same. The 1993 "interview" is only half the length of the 1992 "interview" — one hour. Also, the 1993 interview conspicuously omits any discussion of "Sister Lucy's" alleged statement in 1992 that the Third Secret of Fatima was meant for the Pope, not the Faithful at large.

The 1993 "interview" does contain in substance a repetition of "Sister Lucy's" alleged statements in 1992 that Russia was consecrated in 1984 according to the wishes of Our Lady, and that Russia is now "converting". On this occasion, however, Evaristo resorts to blatantly leading questions in order to prod "Sister Lucy" into giving the answers which would buttress the plainly incredible interview of 1992:

Evaristo:

So it is true that the consecration is done *right*? *true*?

"Sister Lucy":

Yes, it is true ... it is done ...

Evaristo:

And Russia has *started to convert*, *no*?

"Sister Lucy":

Yes, it has started to convert ... the word ... conversion. We should not give ears to those people who say otherwise ... The word conversion ... to convert ... indicates a change. A conversion is a change.

Evaristo:

Yes.

"Sister Lucy":

A change from evil ... It does not indicate that all evil will disappear but just a conversion from evil to good ...

More on the New Meaning of "Conversion"

As we can see from the above quote, in the second pamphlet "Sister Lucy" continues to insist that the conversion of Russia does not require conversion to the Catholic Faith. She will now settle for a supposed "conversion from evil to good."

So, Russia, a land of abortion on demand and vicious discrimination against the Holy Catholic Church, is now *good*? And what about the rest of the world, in which 600 million babies have been slaughtered by abortion since the 1984 "consecration of Russia" — is the rest of the world now undergoing this "conversion from evil to good" as well? Or was the whole world *already* good, given the new meaning of "conversion" invented by the new "Sister Lucy"?

Russia has "*started* to convert"? Has it "started" to spare the lives of its unborn children? Has the world at large "started" to halt the holocaust of abortion? Is the world today more good or less good than it was before the "conversion" of Russia "started" in 1984? Of course, we know the answers to these questions, even if the new Modernist version of "Sister Lucy" does not.

The new "Sister Lucy" tells us that conversion "does not indicate that all evil will disappear". Does not conversion require at least that a nation *stop killing its own children in the womb*? Has "Sister Lucy" forgotten that in 1917, not even communist Russia permitted abortion? Are we now to believe that Russia is "converting" when it is guilty of a routine daily slaughter of innocents which not even the Bolsheviks permitted at first?

Can "Sister Lucy", the sainted seer of Fatima, really be unaware that more innocent lives have been taken by abortion since the 1984 "consecration of Russia" than were claimed in all the wars in the history of the world, including all the wars spawned by Communism, which is only one of Russia's errors? When "Sister Lucy" tells us that not *all* evil will disappear after the conversion of Russia, does she mean to say that a "conversion from evil to good" can coexist with legalized abortion?

We can only be outraged that the "Sister Lucy" presented to us by Mr. Evaristo would apply the word "conversion" to a state of affairs in which the civil authorities of nations around the world, including "converted" Russia, have decreed that children in the womb are not human beings and may be exterminated at will. We can only be sickened by this pollution of the purity of the Message of Fatima.

But the 1993 model of the new "Sister Lucy" has even more to say on the strange new notion of conversion which she introduced for the first time in 1992:

"Sister Lucy":

> "The Holy Father will consecrate Russia to Me which will convert" ... and a conversion is a change of a path of evil to good ... "and there will be some time of peace."

So, Russia is now on the *path to goodness*? And the West too? What exactly do we see on this path to goodness which the new "Sister Lucy" discerns in world events since 1984? We see, first of all, the emerging European Union with its universal abortion on demand, contraception, "legalized" euthanasia, divorce, pornography, prostitution, "gay rights" and empty Catholic churches. If this is the "path of evil to good", what, God forbid, would constitute the path of good to evil? Sacred Scripture solemnly admonishes "Woe to you that call evil good, and good evil ..." [Isaias 5:20] Yet that is precisely what the new "Sister Lucy" has done in Mr. Evaristo's little pamphlet.

We must conclude, therefore, that it could not possibly be the Sister Lucy we know and believe who utters these abominable things. The Sister Lucy who saw the Mother of God at Fatima and the vision of hell Our Lady permitted to her, would never *in any sense* use the word "conversion" or "good" to describe the unprecedented evil which exists in Russia and the rest of the world today.

The New Meaning of Peace

At Fatima, on July 13, 1917, Our Lady promised absolutely:

> "But in the end, My Immaculate Heart will triumph, the Holy Father will consecrate Russia to

Me, Russia will be converted and a period of peace will be given to mankind."

And what of the "period of peace" which Our Lady promised as the fruit of the conversion of Russia? If we have had "a period of peace" since 1984, then how does one explain the incessant war on the unborn, which has claimed 600 million innocent victims since then, or the constant eruption of local and regional conflicts around the globe over the past 14 years?

The Hindu Nationalist government of India has, in early May, 1998, conducted three underground nuclear tests, and the people of New Delhi danced in the streets shouting praise to the Hindu god of war. Pakistan, a Muslim country, has in late May conducted its own nuclear tests in an arms race with India.

This is peace?

But here too "Sister Lucy" finds new meanings for old and well understood words:

"Sister Lucy":

> But this peace to which the Virgin refers in the prophecy refers to wars and persecutions that the errors of atheist communism were causing all over the world ...

Evaristo:

> This is important to get straight ... as this is why many people do not comprehend and think that world peace is to be instantaneous ...

"Sister Lucy":

> The Virgin spoke of a peace from wars promoted by errors ... by the errors of atheist communism in the whole world ... Atheism, yes ... and therefore it is the greatest heresy that exists and it spreads from atheist communism ... it could have been a communism that wasn't atheist ... But it re-

fers to atheist communism that was producing many wars in the whole world.

Evaristo:

Why is there no peace in Russia today? Why?

"Sister Lucy":

Because the wars that exist now are practically not derived from atheism but are civil wars.

So, the new "Sister Lucy" tells us that the peace of the Reign of Mary following the conversion of Russia and the Triumph of Her Immaculate Heart means only that there will no longer be *atheist* wars, but all other wars will continue unabated!

A Friendly New Atheism

But does not atheism still exist in the world today? Are not wars still being fomented by *atheists* around the globe? The new "Sister Lucy" has an answer to this question as well: You see, the atheism of today is a kinder, gentler atheism which does not seek to destroy the Holy Catholic Church! Read it for yourself:

"Sister Lucy":

... atheism still exists but I think *it is no longer the atheism that wanted to destroy the Faith, the Church, God*, and everything that is supernatural.

So, the Faith is no longer threatened by atheism!

Here the strange new "Sister Lucy" jettisons much of the New Testament! St. Paul tells us in Hebrews (11:6), "He who comes to God must believe that God exists and that He rewards those who seek Him." Therefore, atheists will go to hell precisely for their atheism. Did Our Lord Himself not say that those who are not with Him are against Him?[23] Therefore, atheism makes one an enemy of Christ. Did St. Paul not teach that the atheist stands condemned as an enemy of God because he has closed his mind and heart to the evidence of God in nature (Romans 1:18-21) which even a man without faith can see? Is not atheism the very creed that the devil himself promotes? How, then, could atheists be anything but a threat to the Church, given that they are, by definition, Her enemies by the very fact that they are enemies of Jesus Christ and followers of satan's doctrine?

Seeing that atheists are enemies of Jesus Christ, Who is the Head of the Catholic Church, and realizing that atheists follow the lead of satan, how is it possible for any one, even the new "Sister Lucy," to claim that modern-day atheists are not a threat to the Church?

And if this new, kinder atheism no longer seeks to destroy the Church and the supernatural, why is the world today steeped in the death and destruction of both body and soul in godless materialistic societies, which kill babies in the womb by the millions? The new "Sister Lucy" has no answer, because the new "Sister Lucy" is not asked such embarrassing questions. Her questioner, Mr. Evaristo, is evidently interested in preserving the credibility of his new "Sister Lucy", who caused him so much trouble when he first introduced her to the world in his pamphlet of 1992.

This new kind of atheism described by the new "Sister Lucy" must be seen as symptomatic of the general process of apostasy within and without the Church in the post-conciliar period. The destruction of the Roman liturgy, the overturning of our most cherished ecclesial traditions, the loss of vocations, wretched catechisms, the decline in the life of prayer in individuals and communities, have all combined to erode the integrity and the militancy of the Faith.

Did not Our Lord warn us in Sacred Scripture that "you are the salt of the earth but if the salt loses its flavor, of what use is it? It is good for nothing except to be thrown out and trampled underfoot." (Matthew 5:13). This new message of Fatima has no salt and is good for nothing. Only a Catholic who has lost the traditional faith could find it palatable. And for millions of young Catholics today, the new message of Fatima will be palatable only because they have never been fed by the faith of the ages in the first place. These millions of Catholics are the victims of the "new" Church of the post-Vatican II era, with its new message of Fatima — a Church which seems determined to bury its own past.

In view of this pathetic new "message" of Fatima, should we not entreat Rome with all the more urgency to reveal the suppressed Third Secret of Fatima? Cardinal Ratzinger told us in November 1984 that the Third Secret refers to the "dangers which menace the faith and the life of the Christian and therefore (menace) the life of the world."[24]

For if Christians no longer salt the earth with a fervent faith, what will stay the wrath of God? What will keep Christians who have lost their salt from being trampled underfoot, as Our Lord warned?

Many believe that the revelation of the Third Secret would deliver us from the current apostasy, which clearly includes Mr. Evaristo's saltless version of the Fatima message.

Yet Another Fantasy

At the end of the 1993 interview, the new "Sister Lucy" offers another observation about world events which brings to mind the Vatican's dismissal of her fantastic story about Gorbachev's repentance on his knees before the Pope:

"Sister Lucy":

But when [in 1984] we were at the beginning of a nuclear war and all of a sudden (*sic*), those projects for war that the nations had ... From one moment to another at the moment when the Holy Father made the consecration, those projects of war ... Everything changed! and (*sic*) these projects of war ... changed into projects of peace! ... These were projects to terminate everything that have now changed into projects to liberate! ...

Evaristo:

Then, has the era of Peace come, now that the Consecration of Russia has been accomplished and that communism has collapsed?

"Sister Lucy":

The consecration of 1984 prevented an atomic (nuclear) war *that would have occurred in 1985* ...

It is very strange indeed that after "Sister Lucy" offered the observation that a nuclear war would have occurred in 1985 if not for the 1984 "consecration", *not one question was asked* about this remarkable statement. Was not Evaristo concerned about where Sister Lucy had acquired this astounding knowledge of a nuclear war narrowly averted? Yet Evaristo wanted to know nothing about it during the 1993 "interview". This is most curious. Perhaps Evaristo realized that, like the conversion and repentance of Gorbachev, this "revelation" would not bear much scrutiny and was best left unexamined.

At any rate, one searches his memory in vain for any recollection of news stories in 1985 about the imminence of nuclear war between the United States and Russia. Nor does anyone with even a modicum of knowledge about world events over the past 15 years believe for a moment that Russia has stopped producing weapons of mass destruction and turned her energies to "projects to liberate"!

And what "projects of liberation", exactly, is the new "Sister Lucy" referring to? Is she not aware that Russia, along with Israel, is now the chief supplier of weaponry to Communist China,[25] where the Catholic Church has been forced underground and bishops and priests are arrested for the "crime" of being Catholics in union with the Holy See? Is the new "Sister Lucy" unaware that Russia still possesses enough nuclear weapons to destroy the entire world several times over, and that Russian missiles by the thousands remain "on alert" in their silos?

In fact, a major U.S. television news show revealed that in January 1995 Russia came within *two minutes* of a nuclear launch against the United States[26] in response to a false warning on its early warning radars! U.S. Senator Sam Nunn has stated publicly that Russia's nuclear weapons are on a "hair trigger", and that the danger of nuclear war through human error or misjudgment is greater than it ever was during the "Cold War".[26]

None of these hard facts about the state of the world seems to have penetrated the Convent at Coimbra, where the new "Sister Lucy" tells us, through Mr. Evaristo, of a world at peace, on the path of conversion to goodness. Yet we know that the world described by the new "Sister Lucy" is not the world we inhabit. It is a fantasy world, where apostasy is conversion, evil is good and war is peace.

The New Message of Fatima

It would be well to summarize, in conclusion, the new message of Fatima which proceeds from the new meanings given to its key words by the new "Sister Lucy" who speaks to us from the pages of Mr. Evaristo's pamphlets:

The *consecration* of Russia does not mean that Russia needs to be mentioned.

The *conversion* of Russia does not mean that Russia will embrace the Catholic Faith, or indeed any religious faith at all. It means only that Russia will grant "individual choice", just like the godless pluralistic societies of the West. Nor does the *conversion* of Russia mean that Russia will stop killing babies in the womb or grant true liberty to the Catholic Church.

The *peace* which Our Lady promised at Fatima if Russia were converted means only the cessation of wars caused by atheism, but all other wars will continue unabated.

The *atheism* of today is not an enemy of the Holy Catholic Church.

The careful reader will notice that what this new, Modernist message of Fatima promises us is nothing more than a world *in exactly the same condition in which we see it today* — a world of godless, pluralistic societies which murder babies in the womb by the millions, refuse to recognize Christ the King or His Queen Mother, and reject the teaching authority of the Holy Catholic Church.

Yes, by some amazing coincidence, the new message of Fatima in the Evaristo pamphlets jibes perfectly with the *status quo* of the emerging New World Order.

By another amazing coincidence, the new message of Fatima also serves perfectly the Ostpolitik and "ecumenical brotherhood" being promoted with abandon by certain Vatican bureaucrats, who no longer speak of such things as hell, conversion, and the triumph of the Immaculate Heart of Mary.

Some light is shed on this convenient coincidence when we consider that Mr. Evaristo has boasted of his kind treatment by Cardinal Casaroli, chief architect of the new Vatican policy toward Communism and the world's false religions.

At Fatima, Mr. Evaristo could be seen in a gesture of friendship with his highly placed friend in the Vatican. Perhaps this explains how an obscure layman who was a total stranger to Sister Lucy could gain unprecedented access to the last surviving seer of Fatima, while mere Catholic archbishops and bishops are forbidden to speak to her without permission from Cardinal Ratzinger or the Pope himself.

So in this new message of Fatima, the Triumph of the Immaculate Heart and the Reign of Mary become nothing more than universal pluralistic democracy in a non-Catholic "civilization of love" which the Vatican itself is promoting. All is well.

But all is not well. The world grows more rebellious, the signs of the coming Apocalypse more evident, by the hour. Something is terribly wrong with the world. And something is terribly wrong at the convent in Coimbra.

Was it Sister Lucy de Jesus, the last surviving Fatima seer, who spoke to Carlos Evaristo on October 11, 1992, and again on October 11, 1993? It does not matter. For even if the voice did belong to her, the words did not. They are surely not the words of Heaven entrusted to the saintly little girl at Cova da Iria more than 80 years ago; the little girl who was shown the fires of hell and told of the great chastisement which is fast approaching.

This new message of Fatima simply cannot be accepted in good conscience by anyone who holds fast to the traditional Catholic Faith, or indeed to what Sister Lucy herself declared over and over again for seventy-five years before her alleged encounters with Mr. Evaristo. We see in this new message of Fatima all of the confusion and self-contradiction of the arch-heresy of Modernism, which says one thing but means quite another. We see, in fact, precisely what Mr. Evaristo himself admitted was present in the statements of the new "Sister Lucy":

" ... contradictory and unlogical things which at times seem almost *craziness*."[27]

At Fatima Our Lady warned that "if My requests are not granted ... various nations will be annihilated." In a world which seems intent precisely on annihilating itself, which moves ever closer to the divine chastisement it so richly deserves, not only faith but *prudence itself* dictates that we reject what Mr. Evaristo has presented to us as the words of "Sister Lucy" of Fatima.

And so, although we love Sister Lucy and pray for her well-being, with pain in our hearts we must declare the cold, hard truth: We would be fools to believe this new message of Fatima.

Footnotes:
1. *Two Hours with Sister Lucy*, First Ed., 1/1/93; by Carlos Evaristo, p. 8.
2. Letter of Father Francisco Pacheco, O.C.C. Postal, 60.033-790-Fort-CE-Brazil, published in *The Fatima Crusader* magazine, Issue No. 46, p. 15; January 1994.
3. Fax sent by Carlos Evaristo to Coralie Graham, 23 November 1992, p. 2, paragraph (i).
4. Id., par. (g).
5. Id., par. (i).
6. *The Catholic Counter-Reformation in the XXth Century*, October 1996, #289, p. 6.
7. *It All Started with Two Hours with Sister Lucy*, p. 4.
8. Id. pp. 8-9.
9. Written by Father Pierre Caillon and published in *Fidelite Catholique*, April, 1983. B.P. 217-56402, Auray Cedex, France.
10. *Tragedy and Triumph*, Frère François de Marie des Anges, p. 218, see also f.n. #273 on page 233.
11. *L'Osservatore Romano,* Italian Edition, May 12, 1982.

12. *Fatima: Tragedy and Triumph*, Frère François de Marie des Anges, Immaculate Heart Publications, Ed., 1994, pp. 218-219.

13. *Fidelite Catholique*, April 1983 [article written by Fr. Pierre Caillon of Centre Saint Jean 61500 Sees, (Orne) France], B.P. 217-56402, Auray Cedex, France, reprinted in *The Fatima Crusader*, Issue 13-14, October-December 1983, p. 3.

14. *It All Started With Two Hours With Sister Lucy*, p. 59

15. *L'Osservatore Romano*, March 26-27, 1984, pp. 1 & 6.

16. *L'Avvenire*, March 26, 1984.

17. *The Whole Truth About Fatima*, Vol. III, *The Third Secret*, English Ed., by Frère Michel de la Sainte Trinité, 1990, Immaculate Heart Publications, U.S.A., pp. 504-505.

18. The Church's teachings on invincible ignorance, baptism of desire and baptism of blood are beyond the scope of this article. Nevertheless, it ought to be maintained that all those who enter Heaven have achieved in some way a conscious, explicit desire to belong to the Catholic Church and to submit to her authority, even if this occurs only at the moment of death. To deny this is to turn the doctrine of "no salvation outside the Church" into an empty formula — the very thing that Pius XII condemned in his encyclical *Humani Generis*. To hold, as the Modernists do, that Heaven is peopled by "anonymous Christians" who were oblivious to the truth until after death, makes a mockery of God's grace and denies the necessity of explicit Faith for salvation.

19. *Contre-Reformation Catholique*, March 1998; a similar denial by the Vatican was also reported by *Catholic World News Service* on March 2, 1998.

20. "The Catholic Church in Russia", *The Catholic Faith*, March/April 1998 (p. 2).

21. Pontifical Council for Christian Unity Information Service, N. 83, 1993 (II), pages 95-99.

22. *The Whole Truth About Fatima*, Vol. III, *The Third Secret*, by Frère Michel de la Sainte Trinité, English ed., Immaculate Heart Publications, 1990, p. 600.

23. "He that is not with Me is against Me ..." [Matt. 12:30].

24. "I pericoli che incombono sulla fede e la vita del cristiano e dunque del mondo." *Jesus* Magazine, November 11, 1984, published by Society of St. Paul, Milan, Italy, p. 79.

25. Toronto *Globe & Mail*, Apr. 29, 1998, p. A14, A.P. release; A U.S. Congressional report stated, of the $5.3 billion (U.S.) in public arms sales to China between 1990-1996, Russia accounted for approximately 72 percent, or $3.8 billion in sales and the Middle East (mostly from Israel) was responsible for 17

percent (approx. $900 million) of the military sales to China.

26. "Zero Warning", *Sixty Minutes* news show, aired February 8, 1998.
27. Fax sent to Coralie Graham, November 23, 1992.

Appendix IV

PROPOSED ACT
OF CONSECRATION OF RUSSIA
TO THE
IMMACULATE HEART OF MARY

O Most Holy Virgin Mary, Mother of God, Mother of the Church and of each one of us. In response to Pope Benedict XV who in anguish on May 5, 1917 cried out to Thee in the name of the whole Church — asking Thee to show humanity the way of Peace; Thou came to Fatima on May 13, 1917 and subsequently on the 13th of June, July, August, September and October 1917. Thou returned as Thou had promised on June 13, 1929, and revealed that God asks for our act of Consecration of Russia to Thy Immaculate Heart.

Thou said at that momentous vision:

"The moment has come in which God asks the Holy Father to make and to command all the Catholic Bishops of the world to make the Consecration of Russia to My Immaculate Heart, promising to save Russia by this means."

Ever mindful of the words of Jesus that "it is never too late to have recourse to Jesus and Mary" we now, undertake to obey the Will of the Most Holy Trinity revealed to us through Thy words on that day in the Solemn Extraordinary Vision of the Most Holy Trinity and of the Sacrifice of the Mass.

We intend, by the following act of Reparation and of Consecration of Russia to Thy Immaculate Heart, to obey Thy request in the manner that Thou, Our Most Dear and Holy Mother, have requested so that the peace that has been so long desired and which Thou promised may be granted.

We promise in gratitude to Thee and in reparation for all the sins committed in the past and present against Thy Immaculate Heart to promote among all the faithful the pious devotion of the Five First Saturdays of Communions of Reparation to Thy Immaculate Heart as Thou requested.

We know that nothing happens to nations or individuals unless God wills or permits it. Our poor human race is engulfed by evils of every description: including war, murder of the unborn, famine, pestilence and persecution of the Church.

We now turn to Thee, Our Dear Mother and Mediatrix of all Graces — Our Lady of the Rosary, Thou art our only hope for overcoming the evils of our times and the approaching punishments, which we, sinful humanity, so justly deserve. Mindful that, without Thy help, we cannot overcome these evils on our own, we now turn to Thee in humble supplication to beg Thy help.

It is to Thee, the "Woman" predicted in Sacred Scripture (Gen 3,15), Who has the Commission from God — to crush the Serpent's head, the head of satan, who is a murderer and a liar from the beginning. Thou art that same "Woman" Who Jesus addressed from the cross and left to us as His last will and testament as Our Mother (John 19) — and Thou art indeed the same "Woman" spoken of in Chapter 12 of the Apocalypse Who is clothed with the sun and Who at Fatima was clothed with the sun. It is to Thy Immaculate Heart that we consecrate Russia.

We recognize that all authority comes from God, and mindful of the authority God has entrusted to us to "make disciples of all nations" — we, the successors of the Apostles, engage our authority to consecrate a nation. We hereby consecrate Russia to His service through that nation's consecration to Thy Immaculate Heart.

We recognize that great crimes against God have been committed in Russia. Therefore, we offer on this day of prayer, reparation to the Sacred Heart of Jesus and the Immaculate Heart of Mary for the crime of State Atheism, and all the sacrileges and blasphemies that the godless Soviet regime has perpetrated in Russia.

We pray in fraternal solidarity with our brothers and sisters in Russia who have suffered so horribly, who have been persecuted, tortured, imprisoned and killed. We pray that Russia be saved: that it be converted to the holy Catholic Faith, and that it be made a vessel of divine election.

We make this consecration in response to God and to Thee, Our Blessed Lady, and in response to the millions of petitions made by the Faithful everywhere, particularly the requests for this Act of Consecration made by many of the Russian people who indeed are close to our heart.

And we, so that our fervent prayers for conversion of our generation to Jesus Christ the King and that the fervent prayers and aspiration of all the Faithful and in particular the Faithful of Russia may be heard, and to give to Thee, O Immaculate Virgin Mary, the testimony of our devotion and obedience so now we in a most solemn and public manner consecrate, and entrust all the people of Russia to Thy Immaculate Heart, with the firm hope that soon, thanks to the all-powerful patronage of Thee, O Blessed Virgin Mary, the wishes which we form may be happily fulfilled, for a true peace, fraternal concord and the liberty due to all, and in the first place to the Church. Thus by our prayer, united to Thy own and that of the whole Christian people, the Kingdom of the Savior Jesus Christ will be firmly established over all the earth: "A Kingdom of truth and life, a Kingdom of holiness and grace, a Kingdom of justice, love and peace."

And I suppliantly ask Thee, O Most Merciful Mother, to obtain from Thy Divine Son, Heavenly light for our minds and for our souls, the strength and courage by which, being supernaturally upheld, we all will be able to repulse and overcome all errors and impiety. Amen.

Appendix V

The 14 Fatima Resolutions

I/We hereby agree to the Resolutions drafted and agreed to by the bishops, priests and laypeople at the Second Bishops Conference for World Peace held in Mexico City on November 8-14, 1994 as indicated below. I, the undersigned, in my personal capacity, responding to the inspiration of Our Lady of Fatima to work for peace, have read the resolutions that I have signed and agree with each one's doctrinal content and personally undertake to see that truth contained in each resolution be lived and any undertaking stated therein I shall personally do.

In order to bring about peace and proper ordering of man to God as individuals, in society and in the Church, I hereby make the following resolutions and encourage men and women of good will around the world to join us.

1. We the undersigned individual laypeople, priests, bishops, in our personal capacity, hereby profess our loyalty to the Holy Roman Catholic Magisterium and the august person of His Holiness Pope John Paul II and above all to the Catholic Faith as handed down by the dogmatic councils, tradition, and the approved creeds, not limited to but including the Apostle's Creed, the Nicene Creed, the Athanasian Creed, the Creed of the First Vatican Council and the Credo of the people of God of Pope Paul VI and those doctrines taught Magisterially by the Second Vatican Council.

"Magisterially" — That is, those doctrines that are taught infallibly by the Ordinary and Universal Magisterium of the Church in Vatican II documents.

2. We, as loyal Roman Catholics, as expressed above in resolution number one, also believe that world peace will not be brought about except through obedience to the full meaning and message of Our Lady of Fatima.

3. We undertake to do what we can and we believe it is part of our duty of state to bring about the Triumph of the Immaculate Heart of Mary through the specific plans and requests She made to us in the public and prophetic Message of Fatima.

4. It is our duty according to our state to do all we can and tell those we can to thereby make the full message of Our Lady of Fatima known as Jesus Himself has commanded, despite any difficulties.

5. We the undersigned, mindful of Our Lady of Fatima's request, undertake to personally pray the Rosary every day and to strongly promote this devotion to Our Lady, to those around us.

6. We the undersigned, mindful of Our Lady of Fatima's request that we, each of us, wear the Brown Scapular of Mount Carmel, undertake to personally wear the Scapular and to promote the Brown Scapular among the faithful and men of goodwill that God puts on our path.

7. We the undersigned, recognizing that Our Lady of Fatima and God Himself want to establish devotion in the world to the Immaculate Heart of Mary; and further recognizing that Our Lady and Our Lord especially want us to embrace this devotion; we therefore, personally undertake to make the personal act of consecration to Our Lady's Immaculate Heart. We will also promote it to those God puts on our path.

8. Since Jesus and Mary have so ardently desired the practice of the Five First Saturdays and Communions of Reparation to the Immaculate Heart of Mary, we personally undertake to do these Five First Saturdays as requested and explained by Our Lady of Fatima and Jesus

Himself. We also undertake to promote the Five First Saturdays to the faithful Catholics God puts on our path.

9. Since Our Lady of Fatima wants the Third Secret to be published to the world, we the undersigned, until it is officially revealed, will endeavor to read, study and distribute knowledge of the Third Secret — from the best sources available.

10. We also respectfully petition for the release of the actual words of Our Lady's Third Secret according to Her instructions.

11. Since Jesus and Mary in the Fatima Message make it clear that it is only by means of the solemn and public Consecration of specifically RUSSIA, RUSSIA to the Immaculate Heart of Mary by all the Catholic bishops together with the Holy Father on the same day at the same hour, that true peace will be given to the world: we the undersigned undertake to bring about the long desired Act of Consecration. Such actions (to cause this Act of Consecration) are not limited to, but may include: Prayers; Rosaries; Sacrifices offered to Jesus and Mary for this intention; to attend seminars, symposiums, conferences; to hold such conferences to promote this Consecration; to circulate books, videos, audio tapes to laypeople, priests and bishops to promote this Consecration.

12. We the undersigned, will strive to make known those prophecies that as far as we can ascertain, contain parts of the 3rd Secret which are found in Sacred Scripture and in Church approved apparitions, as Cardinal Ratzinger indicated in his interview with Vittorio Messori, published in November 1984 *Jesus* Magazine.

13. Inasmuch as God wants all men to be saved and come to the knowledge of the truth, and inasmuch as in an approved apparition of Our Lady of 1838 — Our

Lady revealed the Green Scapular of the Immaculate Heart of Mary — especially for the preservation among Catholics and the spread of the Catholic Faith to non-Catholics; and inasmuch as God wants to establish devotion to the Immaculate Heart throughout the world; we the undersigned resolve when opportune to propagate as widely as possible among men, women and children of the world, the Green Scapular and encourage others to do the same and to pray the prayer indicated therein for the conversion of all non-Catholics and the preservation of all Catholics in the Catholic Faith which is so necessary in order to save one's soul.

14. That in the light of our desire to please Our Lady, that the Consecration of Russia be renewed on the Feast of the Immaculate Conception — December 8th, each year by the Pope and all the Catholic Bishops of the world; we the undersigned, respectfully ask for this Consecration of Russia to be done on the above date.